DEREK HILL

DEREK HILL
An Appreciation

GREY GOWRIE

QUARTET BOOKS
London   New York

First published by Quartet Books Limited 1987
A member of the Namara Group
27/29 Goodge Street
London W1P 1FD

Copyright © 1987 by the Earl of Gowrie

British Library Cataloguing in Publication Data

Gowrie, Grey
  Derek Hill
  1. Hill, Derek—Criticism and
  interpretation
  I. Title   II. Hill, Derek
  759.2   ND497.H57/

ISBN 0-7043-2598-5

The frontispiece shows Greenport, Tory Island, 1961
oil on canvas   25 × 29 ins   DAVID CLARKE

Design by Namara
Typeset by MC Typeset Limited, Chatham, Kent
Printed in Great Britain by Shenval Print Limited, Harlow, Essex

Dedicated to the memory of Henry McIlhenny

Note on the Captions

Each caption conforms to the following pattern:

Notes to the paintings by the artist
Title of painting   Year of execution
Medium   Dimensions   OWNERSHIP

Dimensions are given in inches; height precedes width. Although every effort has been made to ensure accuracy, certain details have proved impossible to establish beyond doubt. Readers are requested to inform the publishers of any corrections concerning the measurements or present whereabouts of paintings.

Lines from 'The Peninsula' are reprinted by permission of Faber & Faber Limited from *Door into the Dark* by Seamus Heaney.

Contents

Introduction   1
Appraisal   5
Conversation   27
Biographical Note   145
Public Collections Containing
Works by Derek Hill   149
Derek Hill's Principal
One-man Shows   151

Introduction

DEREK HILL'S FAME as a portrait painter has helped to obscure his achievement as a landscape artist. Specifically, and ironically, his fame as a portrait painter of the British Establishment has helped obscure his achievement as the best painter of the Irish landscape since Jack Yeats; indeed to my mind he excels Yeats as a landscape artist pure and simple. His reputation is also obscured by the fact that, as the transcript of our conversations reveals, he does not entirely earn his living by painting. Hill has painted for forty years with deepening absorption in his craft. His relative financial independence has kept him from wooing the public wholeheartedly. He has not attached himself to a dealer with a stake in promoting his work; the result is not many shows, and not many notices. He has sold some of his best paintings, the Irish landscapes, but these mainly to friends or serious Hill collectors. Nevertheless, his pictures are to be found among the great collections of the world. He is a notable art collector himself, like two other fine British painters of the previous generation, Edward le Bas and Lord Methuen. He is also rather unprofessionally free of jealousy in respect of other artists and has always purchased work he admires or feels may be neglected.

The aim of this book is not just to introduce Derek Hill's work to a wider public; I'm afraid the cost of colour reproductions rather precludes that. It is to demonstrate to those who care about contemporary painting in general, and British painting in particular, that as well as a fine portraitist who has given us a peculiarly fascinating social record, we have in Hill a master of landscape, a leading twentieth-century painter in this field. There are not that many works included here to support this contention, but there are enough.

Reference to contemporary painting may puzzle some readers. Even those who know and like Hill's work tend to think of him as a conservative painter, influenced by the nineteenth century: the early and mid nineteenth century of Constable, Corot and Courbet rather than the Impressionists or post-Impressionists. Neither the twentieth-century modernist mainstream nor the ebb and flow of post-war development known as contemporary art is at first glance suggested by Hill's intense paintings of the west of Ireland. My brief introductory essay makes the case for a second glance. Aspects of the modern, of the contemporary even, emerge in Hill's best pictures and allow him a definite contribution to the art of his own time.

There is another, more personal motive for the book. I earn my living in the art market – a commercial market of great variety and fascination – and have done so, with political interruptions, for many years. Vicarious, even pecuniary contact with works of art seems magical to me. As a child, even at the age when most children produce bright, lively near-Matisses or Dufys, my efforts were brown overlaid with khaki. I was so abnormally untalented myself at any kind of drawing, painting or modelling that the plastic world has ever since been a source of wonder, untinged by envy or sense of missed personal opportunity. Artists inhabit an ever-brave new world to me, and I know how lucky I am to be allowed to sell tickets in their arena.

In my early teens I became a neighbour of Derek Hill in Donegal.

More than anyone he helped define my own interests in the visual arts, letting me ride home across the bog roads with loaned Henry Moore maquettes in my knapsack. Another neighbour was Henry McIlhenny, whose home in Philadelphia contained the collection he founded while a student at Harvard during the Depression. There were paintings by Chardin, David, Ingres, Degas, Renoir, Cézanne, Seurat, Toulouse-Lautrec, Van Gogh and all were masterpieces: the most idiosyncratic and interesting collection of great French painting in the United States. His castle in Donegal was hung, just after the war, with pre-Raphaelites and Landseers: an astonishing taste for a lover of French painting at that time. Henry died in 1986; Derek and I would like to dedicate this collection of Hill reproductions to his memory, not least because he introduced Derek to Donegal.

Both McIlhenny and Hill were formidable mentors and the three of us shared a passion for their adopted and my native country. To any charge that personal considerations such as these lessen objectivity, I have to answer that objectivity isn't always the ideal quality to bring before a work of art, at least at an early stage, and this book is by way of being an introduction to Derek Hill. I am confident, too, that such a charge will not stand up to scrutiny of the paintings themselves.

Quartet have done their best to make this initial scrutiny acceptable and I, who know the paintings in the flesh, so to speak, think they have done very well. I must acknowledge with gratitude their help in the production of the book: it is easier to write about paintings than to reproduce them accurately. Nevertheless, I hope that the reader will realize that he is, in a sense, *reading* these paintings rather than looking at them: looking is a much more complex physical response. I hope he will seek them out in the flesh as well and that more museums and galleries will over the years enable him to do so. That would make the work that has gone into this selection worthwhile. It is of course just that: not a comprehensive catalogue but a selection for which I alone am responsible.

After choosing the works for reproduction, I meant to incorporate biographical material into what would have been a much longer introductory essay. To this end I spent three days in all in the artist's company, at his studio in London and at my home in Wales. We talked with decreasing self-consciousness in front of the tape recorder. When I read the transcripts I felt they were more interesting and revealing as foreground rather than background. They seemed like a sketch for a verbal self-portrait, to be set against the impressive melancholy painting reproduced on the dustcover of the book. I felt that anyone attracted to the paintings through the reproductions might well be interested in learning about the artist through the tapes. It seemed a direct and unfiltered way to proceed and it also meant less of me and more of Hill, the point and purpose of the work. It allowed the introductory essay to be short: I like art criticism that tries at least to be pithy – aphoristic, almost – and comes to an end before the boredom and absurdity of translating visual experience into verbal analysis set in.

I have edited the transcripts extensively. Otherwise the text would have overwhelmed the pictures. I wanted to achieve flow and to avoid conversational repetitions, um-ing and er-ing and their linguistic equivalents. But I have tried very hard not to cheat. The sequence is accurate. The words spoken were spoken or implied. They seem to me to be more self-revealing than self-serving. Hill has had a privileged, interesting and fulfilled life. Like most lives, not especially artists' lives but of special importance in their case, it has been difficult and painful as well.

Appraisal

DEREK HILL'S TALENT and competence as a painter were never in doubt. Edward Molyneux, the couturier, was right to edge him away from a career in stage design and towards the lonelier life in front of an easel. It took a long time, however, for Hill to achieve that blend of style and vision which distinguishes the artist from the painter.

Definitions are difficult, but all works of art, surely, must satisfy one criterion in order to deserve the name. They must be unique and universal. As we read or look or listen we need to be able to identify something original, with its own stylistic personality, and recognize something general. The last quality is what allows us to say, 'There! That's it. That's the real thing.' Even an uncompromisingly abstract painting, unconnected with real life as we perceive it, needs a different kind of reality, an object-life of its own.

Some artists arrive very quickly at the stage where a complex and pleasurable response to the art-life equation comes into play (art must always give pleasure). Getting there is part of their talent; the struggle is about ends rather than means, the uses to which talent may be put.

Others progress slowly, learning on the job, so to speak; feeling their way through the conventions of their craft until they arrive at what makes them original. Derek Hill is one of these.

Forty years ago, when Hill started painting seriously and began to think of himself as a painter not a stage designer, there was no evidence that his best work would be landscape. Molyneux was first attracted to a portrait head, and in the early fifties, when Hill spent winters at Berenson's villa above Florence, Berenson himself and Kenneth Clark admired the paintings of olive pruners. This was the time, too, of the very fine Berenson portrait. It seemed likely that the socially ubiquitous Hill would develop as a painter of people. So of course he has, becoming, in my view, the most proficient and appealing of contemporary British portrait painters. But neither the early landscape paintings of France, nor the more assured Tuscan landscapes of the Berenson period, show promise of the real depth and originality of nearly all the Irish work, the paintings of Tory Island in particular.

'What is strange,' wrote Monk Gibbon in 1963, 'is that someone like Derek Hill, a humanist with a keen love of social contacts, should have discovered in one of the bleakest and most remote corners of Western Europe the seascape and landscape theme which many people consider has led him to complete artistic fulfilment.' Against odds, Hill uncovered a seam in his life and personality which allowed him to move from prose to poetry, as it were, and translate his technical skills into art.

The odds were considerable and so they remain. Hill's output of significant paintings is not very large. As our conversations reveal, he is, in a more complicated way than is the case with most people, both a social and a solitary being. This is really the story the book tells and the pictures make the point more profoundly than the words. The story is not just about the claims of the world and the claims of artistic ambition, the usual tussle. Hill needs to paint portraits. Painting portraits is the way, not the only way but perhaps the most profound one, in which he establishes close contact with other individuals. His

An olive pruner on the Berenson estate in Tuscany.

Olive pruner, *c*. 1952   *oil on canvas*   39½ × 47 *ins*
LADY AMABEL LINDSAY

Another pruner on the same estate.
Olive pruner, c. 1952 *oil on canvas 39½ × 18 ins*
MRS BARRY BLACK

sitters nearly always become, and remain, very attached to him. Allowing for the occasional lapse of one who paints five or six portraits a year, Hill is good at likeness. Likeness springs from personality rather than physiognomy: dead people look different. Hill's portraits are not commissioned. They are encounters, relationships. This gives them strengths in terms of portraiture without necessarily guaranteeing them originality as paintings or uniqueness as works of art.

A paradox of Hill's art is its humility before the subject, the way he arrives at a style which contains rather little of his own personality, or more accurately, little of the side most people see. 'I do like to talk while painting people. It relaxes me and it relaxes them. It allows the personality to come through. I need to be able to see the personality coming through; it's a tangible, a visible thing, something that happens while you talk.'

If Hill's empathy for his sitters is one of the reasons his portraits usually succeed within the limits they set themselves, the obliteration of his own personality may be another. This puts him somewhat outside the mainstream of contemporary painting: obliteration of the artist's personality is not the first thing that comes to mind in respect of twentieth-century art. So humility, objectivity of this kind is difficult to attain. Most of Hill's sitters are well-known people. They come from an Anthony Powell world where the British upper classes, influential still, mix with an equally influential artistic intelligentsia, the mixture occurring, sometimes, within the same individuals. Hill paints people very much as individuals, not types. Unlike Powell he has no satirical talent or gift for irony. Although he is a witty and entertaining companion he is only occasionally humorous in paint. The magnificent portrait of Lord Hailsham is an exception, but the humour is also sympathetic in this case to the sitter, uncovering a personality which combines ebullience with melancholy.

As we admire the tact and objectivity which informs the Hailsham and other portraits, we have to recognize that such qualities, even when graced by technical skill, are unlikely to generate high art very often.

John Dixon, the fisherman brother of James Dixon, the naïf Tory Island artist. John also painted about five pictures during his lifetime, in an entirely different style from his brother.

John Dixon, c. 1972   *oil on canvas*   26 × 26 ins   DAVID CLARKE

To make works of art out of his paintings, Hill needed a different kind of encounter. His career was respectable, not more, until he found one.

For besides technical skill, works of art need tension. Like tragedy, which most people think is the highest form of art, they may require tension in order to overcome it. Painting is of all the arts the one which allows us to share the perception of the artist; it is only just a metaphor to say that painting hits us in the face. We have a product, a physical thing in front of us, which the painter saw that way: we are, again almost literally, in possession of someone else's eyes. This is exciting, because perception, our sense of reality and existence, is altogether bound up with seeing, or with hearing people talk about what they see. It can also be quite threatening, because how we see is a big part of our sense of identity. No wonder we get cross or upset when a painting reorders our perception: books take longer to do so and the world of music, moving or unsettling as it may be, is a place apart.

Nor are we seeing things, simply, through the artist's eyes: we may suspect him of entering or invading our own. Landscape painting is especially close to the psychology of perception. It is surely no coincidence that as culture becomes more and more urban, landscapes allow us to mix memory and desire and put ourselves, to borrow the old military term, in the picture. At first glance this may elicit sympathy for the painter, because most people are attracted to landscapes. In any exhibition of amateur painting idyllic rural scenes make up the bulk of the work. He is nevertheless presented with a difficulty. Because the nature of perception, the painter's and other people's, is intimately connected with attitudes to landscape (I was going to write 'nature' but of course they are not always the same thing as most landscapes are the products of civilization), it becomes all too easy for him to present the viewer with some flattering rehearsed response or, just as bad, a gimmicky effort to see things from a novel or startling angle. Landscape painting all too easily falls into banality or novelty and neither is useful for art.

There is drama in the way Hill overcame this. He no   →14

11

Archbishop John Charles McQuaid of Dublin. Simon Elwes painted him in cerise cardinal robes sitting in a baroque gold chain. I saw him as more severe – standing in black – an almost Renaissance figure. Beneath his well-known forbidding exterior I found a warm-hearted man of understanding and sympathy.

The Most Rev. Dr John Charles McQuaid, Archbishop of Dublin, Chairman of St Vincent's Hospital, 1970 *oil on canvas* 47½ × 40½ ins
ST VINCENT'S HOSPITAL, DUBLIN

Ploughing with oxen in Le Marche province – near the sea.

Ploughing with oxen in Le Marche province, c. 1956 *oil on canvas* 36 × 20 ins
DOUGLAS SEALY

doubt did so unconsciously and luck, as always, played its part. He chose to live in a part of the world that had not been painted very much, or not by professional painters: the north-west corner of Ireland. For a long time his painting did not substantially change. Sunlit Tuscany gave way to the broken light of the Atlantic. Rural faces looked rather the same: I didn't feel especially foolish when, on one occasion, I mistook a picture of three women watching a religious procession from a window in Pompeii for Donegal people. The landscapes remained both classical and modern through the underlying abstraction, the geometric harmony, of the composition. The shifting, unignorable weather of Donegal provided a romantic overlay; as with Constable's sketches, light would spill on to the painting, interrupting the composition in a manner both dramatic and naturalistic. (This is the real romantic thing: W.H. Auden speaks of Goethe's 'passion for weather and stones'.) But for all the skill and seductiveness of these 'tiny postcard masterpieces', as Henry McIlhenny called them, something was missing. Like the landscape, the paintings were very beautiful. They relied a little too much on the look of Donegal and on the associations with other landscape paintings which that kind of scenery provides. There was something formulistic about such perfect mixing of Constable and Corot: John's eye for the weather, Jean-Baptiste's pictorial discipline. Compared with most landscape painting of the fifties and sixties such criticism is still high praise, and it is intended to be. Nevertheless, there remained a distance for Hill to travel before the paintings achieved a maturity of their own, independent of scenic or artistic preconceptions.

The distance turned out to be about eight miles off the Donegal coast. The island of Tory is wild in legend: in the eighteenth century its supposedly savage inhabitants provided an abusive nickname for Whig opponents to hurl at the fledgling Conservative party. In our time, the islanders are a stoic but steadily diminishing community dependent on fishing, government grants and remittances from emigrant, mainly American, relations. Derek Hill is accepted and admired on Tory. →18

Three women watching a religious procession in Pompeii,
c. 1953   *oil on canvas*   24 × 30 ins   MRS BARRY BLACK

A concert performance in Florence. The picture was bought by Mrs Ambrose Chambers so I always called it 'Chamber music'. My favourite concert picture.

Chamber music, c. 1953 *oil on canvas*   7 × 14 ins   PRESENT OWNER UNKNOWN

Yehudi Menuhin came over to be painted in my studio in Donegal. The night we had a ceilidh in the kitchen and the locals all came and also played their fiddles. My housekeeper was later asked what name the famous 'fiddler' had and, acknowledging she was bad at names, she said she thought it was Hewdie McMenamin.

Yehudi Menuhin preparing the Delius Violin Concerto for recording, 1977
oil on canvas   19½ × 29 ins   YEHUDI MENUHIN, OM

He helped create a school of painters there and was successful in putting them on the map nationally and internationally. But his own work is not only drawn from the life of the island. It looks back at the Donegal mountains, impressive across the ocean passage to Gortahork on the mainland. (Some people have compared these paintings to Paul Henry, the Irish painter best known for landscapes of the west. To me they have greater subtlety and strength. They do not appear to be a kind of propaganda for isolation: Henry always seems to have one eye on how his paintings will reproduce on the bedroom walls of exile.) It looks out and around at the Atlantic, celebrating that light which binds Cornwall and Mayo and Maine together: salmon-silvery greys, an olive green occurring both on land and sea, irruptions of deep purple and blue. I believe that Derek Hill has caught this light better than anyone except the nineteenth-century American master, Winslow Homer. He gets it right because on visit after visit to Tory he has given it the same concentration which in our conversation he describes Morandi giving to the veiled light that seems to surround his mundane still lifes with a kind of halo. Painting is all about looking and sculpting what you see.

Sculpture is a precise term in this context. The other great appeal of oil painting, over and above its connection with the eye and sensibility of the painter, is its physicality. The term 'plastic' is part of the jargon of art criticism in its original sense of something being made or moulded. You don't bake a picture, like a pot, or mould it like a sculpture, but you do build it up from its mineral constituents: the stuff of oil paint, the muck. In the landscape painting of the Romantic and post-Romantic era, usually called Modern to distinguish it from Contemporary, the best artists have remained true to the integrity of the raw material. Constable, Turner, Courbet, Monet, Van Gogh all have this in common. The great paintings of Mont St Victoire by Cézanne have the same air of being built up from the ground. Much of the appeal must lie, in an unmetaphysical age, with the analogies which oil paint offers to the physical world of nature. The introduction of white animates the goo on the canvas, giving it, to be metaphysical

Berenson in bed being read to in the morning by Nicky Mariano, still in her red dressing-gown. Nicky left this picture back to me when she died.

Nicky Mariano reads to Bernard Berenson, 1950
oil on board   13 × 16 ins   THE ARTIST

19

for a moment, its genesis of life and light. The analogy works best with landscape; flesh needs a more subtle dilution of the ingredients and the world's supreme paintings have to do with flesh.

On Tory Island Derek Hill found the appropriate physical base for his talent. The exposed rocks and cliff faces gave him geometry and structure and his Bauhaus training let him seize the opportunity they offered. The pitiful, thin soil (generations of islanders have stripped most of what there is for fuel) gave colour. The north Atlantic gave the dance and drama of its light. These paintings lift Hill's career from decent distinction to a sphere where he can compete with his great exemplars, Constable, Corot, Courbet and Morandi. To my eye he wins an impressive number of rounds. The Tory pictures do him honour also in his adopted country. Ireland is famous for poets, not painters. In his best work, Derek Hill brings to canvas the intelligence and passionate observation which Seamus Heaney brings to the printed page.

Now recall

The glazed foreshore and silhouetted log,
That rock where breakers shredded into rags,
The leggy birds stilted on their own leg,
Islands riding themselves out into the fog,

And drive back home, still with nothing to say
Except that now you will encode all landscapes
By this: things founded clean on their own shapes,
Water and ground in their extremity.

The first landscape I remember painting in Donegal, of Mount Errigal, during the summer of 1949, when guest at Glenveagh Castle.

Mount Errigal, 1949 *oil on cardboard*   10 × 14 ins   THE ARTIST

Painted looking towards Donegal Bay from Classiebawn Castle, which Lord Mountbatten had lent me for two weeks when, due to storms, I was unable to reach Tory Island. This picture formerly belonged to Mrs Ailsa Mellon Bruce, who bought four of my Donegal landscapes at my first New York exhibition.

Storm over Donegal Bay, 1960 *oil on cardboard* 6 × 4 ins THE ARTIST

A small, very early morning picture, like the jacket, and done from almost the same spot – I called it Golgotha.

Golgotha, c. 1969 *oil on canvas* 6 × 4 ins THE ARTIST

Painted on an old bit of asbestos board found near my Tory Island hut.

The quiet wave, c. 1978   *oil on asbestos*   *7 × 14 ins*   THE ARTIST

Golgotha II: Tory Sunrise, c. 1978 *oil on canvas* 10 × 19 ins DAVID CLARKE

A concert at the Snape Maltings in honour of Princess Margaret of Hesse and the Rhine. The picture, reproduced in the Festschrift compiled for Peter Pears' seventieth birthday, is now in the Hesse Darmstadt collection.

A concert at the Snape Maltings, 1984 *oil on canvas* 11 × 14 ins
THE HESSE DARMSTADT COLLECTION

Boats pulled up by the Tau cross at West Town, Tory Island. Currachs are still used on the island but the last coracles were abandoned around twenty years ago.

The Tau cross at West Town, 1963 *oil on canvas*   31 × 45 *ins*   THE ARTIST

Conversation

Derek, we've talked together about pictures and paintings for many years in private and now I'm going to turn on a tape and talk with you in public. This is always a rather artificial, or rather art-less thing to do, but I believe that many people who look at the reproductions of your work in this book, getting a sense of it perhaps for the first time, are going to be interested in listening to you, so to speak. To give us something to latch on to, a structure, these conversations will keep coming back to a handful of themes: Ireland and your landscape paintings; portraits and sitters; other painters; collecting; yourself and your life. Let's start with the hardest thing. Can anyone talk truthfully about himself? Can you?

We all deceive ourselves but it is important to try not to. I try not to. It is particularly important for an artist because art is about the truth as you see it and the work shows up anything that isn't the truth.

You seem to me to be a very good painter. But you are not as well known as you deserve to be. Do you mind this?

I don't think I feel neglected as a painter, or disappointed in the way I've been treated. I may have neglected myself; I mean I've never really pushed my work or advertised myself. But I've been well treated all my life. I've been able to paint, my works are in major museums, they are owned by some of the greatest collectors and owners of works of art anywhere. I've had exhibitions and now there is this book.

Your friends, even the most devoted ones, think of you as quite a sensitive or chippy person, one who can take offence quite easily. You don't feel slighted?

I mind some things. The National Portrait Gallery, for instance. I've always found it odd that here I am, quite a decent portrait painter and one who has painted a large number of fascinating people, people of historical significance, and yet the National has got only one portrait of mine, of Anthony Eden, and that only because Clarissa Eden gave it to them.

It's a very good Eden, a head as I remember, quite small.

Yes. I don't think of it as a particularly good portrait head. I mean I'd much rather they had the Michael Tippett or the Wilfrid Thesiger which I think really good. They refused the Tippett. They refused the Thesiger. When they refused one of Lord Crawford I just gave up. I mind all that. But I cheer myself up with the thought that they appear to dislike Augustus John's portraits as well, some of which I think marvellous.

I believe that the reason you are less well known than you should be is that you don't have a dealer. And you don't have a dealer because you don't like to sell your work. Rather the reverse. Is it true that when your pictures come up at auction you buy them back?

Yes. The landscapes nearly always. Sotheby's and Christie's keep an eye

Yehudi Menuhin conducts at King's Lynn in St Nicholas' Church concert. Picture formerly owned by Mrs John Hay Whitney and given to the present owner.

Yehudi Menuhin conducts, c. 1964 *oil on cardboard* 3 × 5 ins
MRS BRAGIOTTI-ETTING

I tried to make this picture show a strong, almost Roman senatorial aspect of Sir Michael Tippett and I consider it one of my best male 'heads'.
It had been intended for the National Portrait Gallery, but when Sir Michael's secretary took it there 'they were not prepared to see it or purchase it'. I then gave it as a present to Sir Michael. The National Portrait Gallery at once commissioned another artist to depict him.

Sir Michael Tippett, OM, c. 1984 *oil on canvas* 18 × 18 ins
SIR MICHAEL TIPPETT, OM

out for me and I usually get them when they do come up. It isn't that I find having a dealer demeaning or something. People who write books don't find it demeaning to have a publisher, though I suppose that is different because books are reproduced. It is simply that I don't always want or need to sell. You may be right about the effect.

What about the portraits?

I never accept commissions. I say to someone, 'I'd like to paint your portrait. Then, if you want to, you can buy it. If not, don't worry.' The same with institutions, though of course they usually start by asking me to paint someone, the head of a college for instance. But I don't think it's fair making people buy pictures, pictures they've asked for even, if they don't want to buy them — all that awful business of the picture being hung in the loo until one comes to lunch when it's hauled out and hung self-consciously in the drawing room. I don't want that at all.

The key phrase, I think, is that you don't need to sell. This is an age of the professional painter, with all the marketing and promotional technique the term implies. You are a highly professional painter in terms of competence, but if you don't sell your work you don't give enough other people, other professionals, a stake in its success. Success has a lot to do with promotion.

You are probably right. But as I said, I don't feel neglected and I know how lucky I am to be able to paint mainly for love. I am, as you know, a collector of works of art and I recognize that an artist needs collectors. There are two really serious collectors of my work, one in England and one in Ireland. I have an important relationship with them both. I see them regularly and I am devoted to them. And the people who buy my portraits do provide me with quite an important part of my living.

What about childhood? I never hear you talk much about your origins. Your

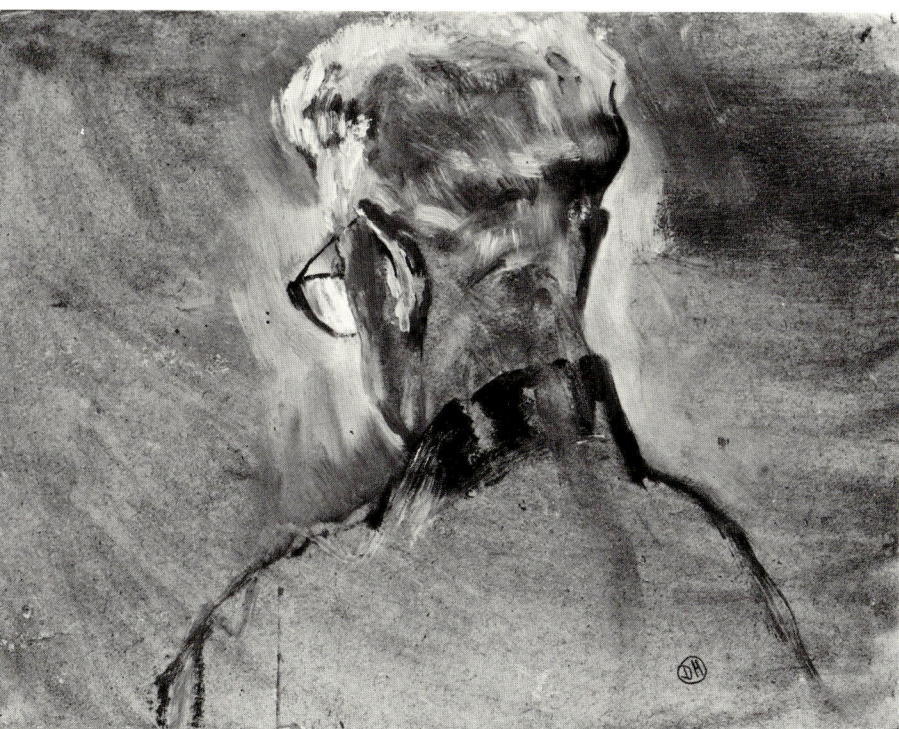

Julian Bream in my Hampstead studio when still a boy. He would arrive in an old van with a rolled-up mattress in the back where he often slept after his country concerts.

Julian Bream, 1950 *oil on canvas* *12 × 18 ins* JULIAN BREAM

The back of Arthur Rubinstein's head painted during the week I stayed with him behind Marbella. One of my happiest painting periods, when the maestro played continually for me and I did four pictures of him in all, plus another of his hands playing. This head that I kept goes to his daughter on my death.

Sketch of Arthur Rubinstein, c. 1972 *oil on canvas* *9⅜ × 12½ ins* THE ARTIST

31

family was prosperous?

Yes. There were servants and gardeners and so on, common enough in those days among the middle class. I have always had enough money to live on and I don't really need all that much, with no wife or children. You must remember that it is only recently that life has become so expensive. I bought my house and its huge garden in Ireland for a thousand pounds in the early fifties which was very cheap even then, even though that thousand pounds would be worth ten or fifteen today. The pictures I collected cost pounds or hundreds of pounds, not thousands. Do you like my portrait of Lord Mountbatten? That has some significance for me as he loved the west of Ireland and of course died there. Our childhood home was at Romsey, a dower house which we rented from the Mountbatten estate.

Were your parents artistic?

No, but they had appreciation. Father won a prize at Marlborough, a drawing prize. And my mother was very musical. Unfortunately, my father not only didn't like music, he actively *dis*liked it. Though my mother could play the violin rather well she felt she shouldn't play after she married. I'd take her to concerts whenever I could, and to Glyndebourne. Music has been important in my own life, both as a painter and when I used to design for the stage.

I admire your paintings of musicians playing, your only conversation pieces really. And the Menuhin and Tippett portraits and the Rubinstein sketch are first-rate. But what were your parents like?

Father was well known as a cricketer. He was A.J.L. Hill: he was Captain of Hampshire and had played with W.G. Grace. He was a businessman. He was involved in shipping coal from Newcastle to Southampton and he had a cloth business at Frome. Mother → 48

The Gamble brothers ploughing beneath St Columb's in Donegal. This field was in cultivation for only two years during my thirty years' residence in the house.

The Gamble brothers ploughing, c. 1960   *oil on canvas*   27½ × 35½ ins
LADY AMABEL LINDSAY

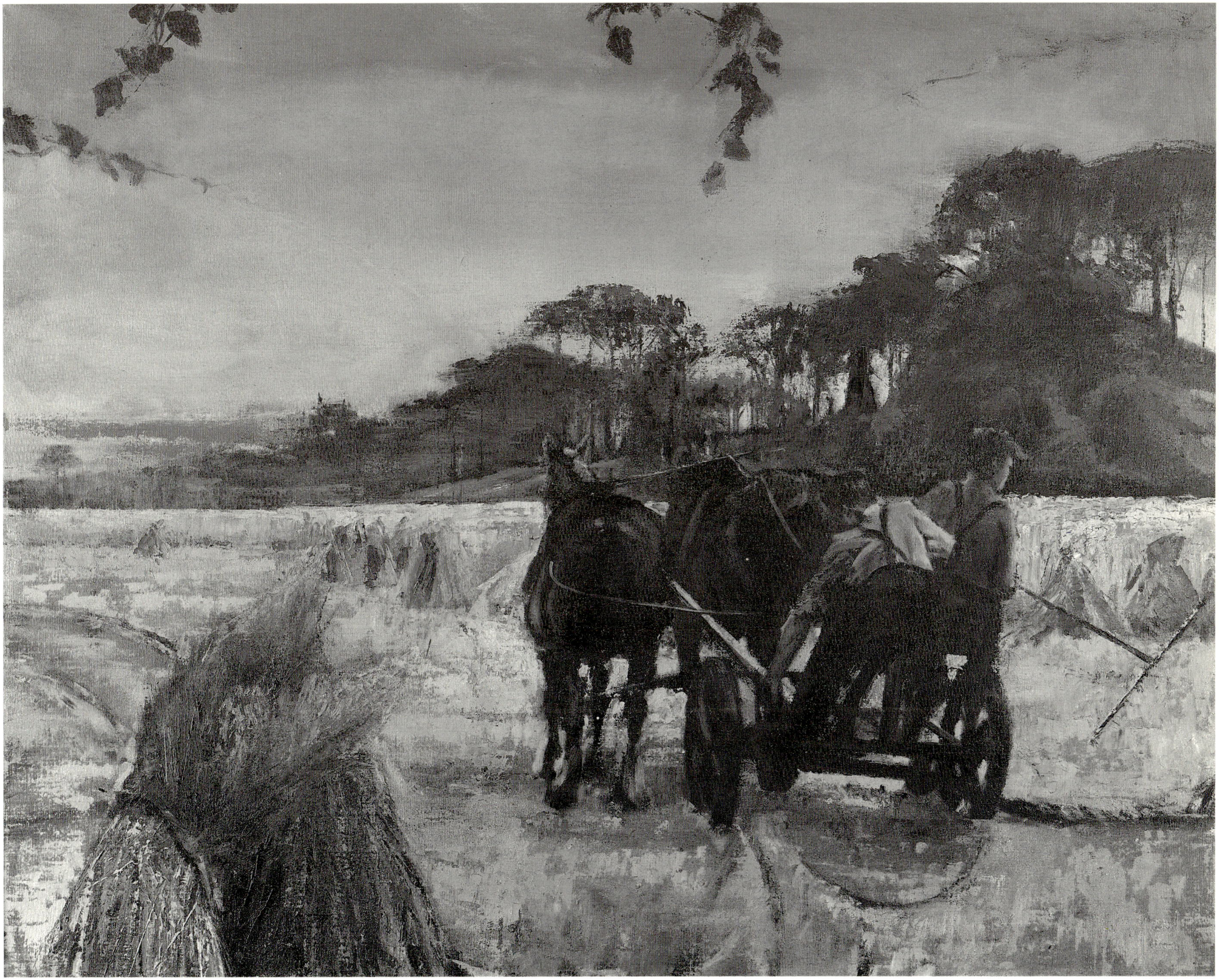

Evening light on Greenport rocks from near my hut – Muckish Mountain on the mainland in the distance. A similar panel, with a rising full moon in the distance, I called 'Homage to Paul Henry'.

Evening light on Greenport rocks, c. 1984   *oil on wood (cigar box)*   4 × 6 ins
THE ARTIST

My largest Tory Island landscape – painted on the school easel that had to be weighted down by rocks to prevent its descent into the gully below. From the north, beyond the gully, is West End Village with the round tower and, beyond again, across Tory sound, the mainland.

The back of Tory Island, 1960   *oil on canvas*   *60 × 48 ins*   THE BANK OF IRELAND

Goose Hill – so called because on this hill the barnacle geese gathered each night when I went to help ring them on the Inishkea islands off County Mayo. One of my favourite small landscapes.

Goose Hill, *c.* 1980   *oil on cardboard*   3 × 4 ins   THE ARTIST

My sole essay into a pointillist technique. Painted from near Sir Walter Scott's view over the Tweed, showing the Eildon Hills beyond.

The Eildon Hills, *c.* 1958   *oil on canvas*   14 × 20 ins
THE EARL HAIG

Building at the Kibbutz on the Sea of Galilee, Ein Gev, where Teddy Kollek, Jerusalem's splendid mayor, sent me for a week when I was guest of the city of Jerusalem for three months.

Building at Ein Gev Kibbutz on the Sea of Galilee, c. 1976   *oil on canvas*
14 × 20 ins   THE ARTIST

Perhaps my favourite Tuscan landscape – south-east of Florence near
Tavernelle – a spring morning of clearness and happiness.

Tavernelle, c. 1950   *oil on canvas*   8½ × 14 ins   ANTHONY HILL

The first head of Bernard Berenson done at I Tatti, his Settignano villa, and commissioned by Sylvia Sprigge who wrote a book on Berenson.

Bernard Berenson, 1953 *oil on canvas*   11 × 20 *ins*   ROBERT SPRIGGE

Cardinal Heard, usually known as a dour Scotsman who lived in Rome and was part of the Vatican 'Rota'. One morning he arrived at the sitting with a twinkle, rubbing his hands. When asked why, he replied: 'Your Dublin Archbishop has just had a bad hour with His Holiness.' He sat for me in a corridor that looked out over a swimming pool where the young college novices were enjoying themselves. Hence his rather sad and wistful smile.

Cardinal Heard, 1965 *oil on canvas* *50 × 40 ins*
MASTER AND FELLOWS OF BALLIOL COLLEGE, OXFORD

Two small panels from pencil drawings done when waiting for the early-morning boat on Mount Athos – a retreat I try hard to reach every year. A period of peace and tranquillity which, like the periods on Tory Island, is absolutely necessary to me.

Waiting for the boat on Mount Athos, c. 1980 *oil on wood* *8¼ × 6 ins , 8¼ × 8¼ ins*
RICHARD CAVENDISH

Eddie Moore, my old Donegal gardener, to whom I was devoted and whose work was responsible for the well-known gardens at St Columb's. They are now owned by the Irish Nation.

over, left
Eddie Moore, 1972 *oil on canvas* *24 × 28 ins* THE ARTIST

Erskine Childers was the first Irish President ever to visit Tory Island and I took him and his wife Rita over to the island when they were staying with me in Donegal. We toured the island on a tractor and I decided to paint my posthumous picture of him relaxed and among local people he knew and understood. The 'powers that be' and his family, however, wanted an official boardroom-type of portrait so this picture was removed from the presidential residence.

over, right
Erskine Childers, President of Ireland, 1974 *oil on canvas* *36 × 39¾ ins*
COMMISSIONERS OF PUBLIC WORKS IN IRELAND

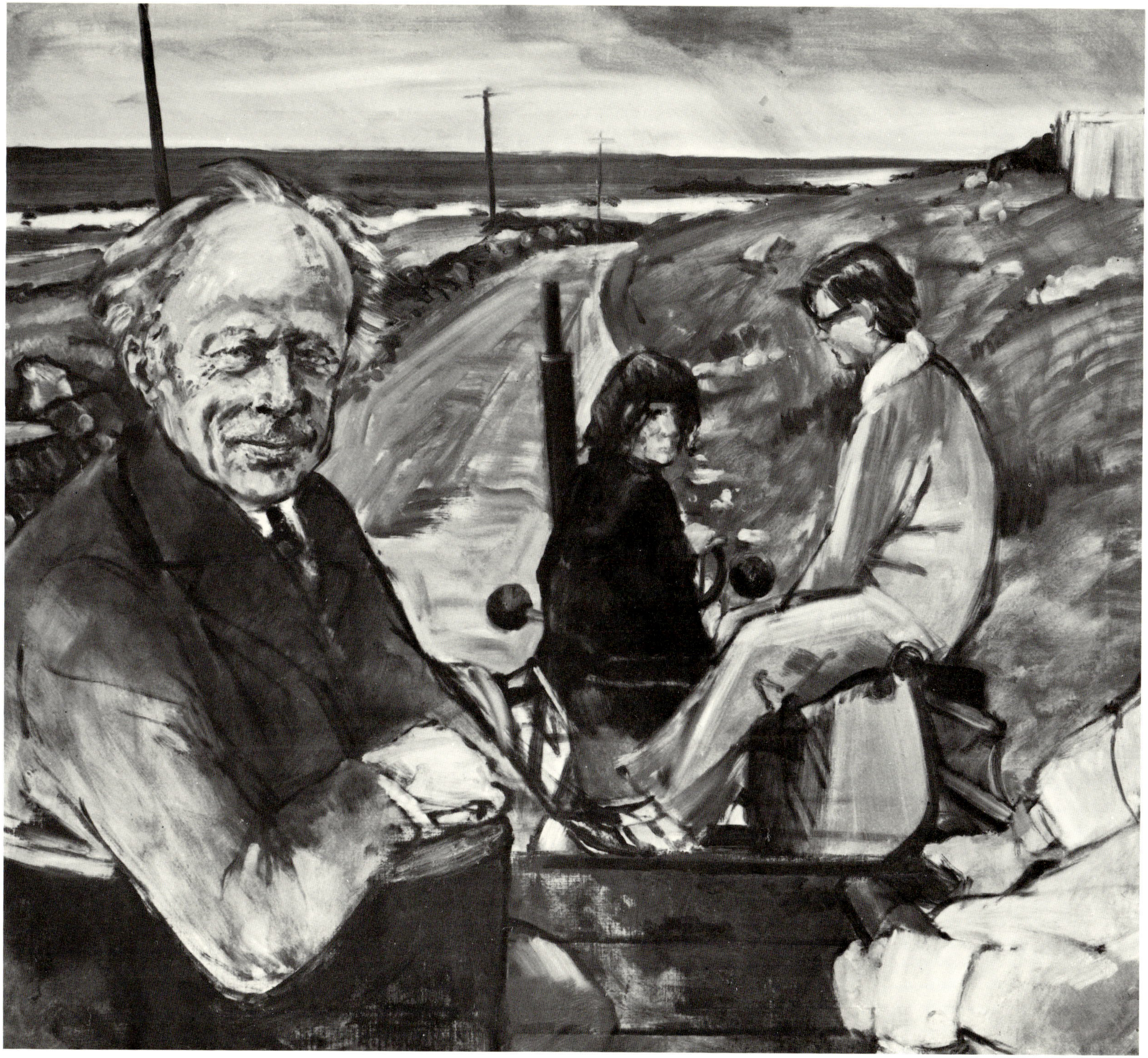

My late Donegal neighbour.

Henry P. McIlhenny, c. 1960 *oil on canvas* *23 × 30 ins*
PHILADELPHIA MUSEUM OF ART

Lord Anthony Hamilton, an Irish neighbour, relaxing at Barons Court.

Lord Anthony Hamilton, 1968 *oil on canvas* *24 × 30 ins*
THE DUKE OF ABERCORN

47

and Father were born in the 1870s and died in the 1950s. It was a very close marriage: too high a standard for me perhaps. Mother was a Mercer. They were Quakers and had a brewery in Weymouth.

And you got on with them?

Yes, very well. Extremely well, which was extraordinary considering Father was interested only in hunting – not hunting, really, but shooting and fishing. He adored both. He was a great sportsman and then of course he played cricket so well. I was a misfit. I didn't like any of those things, particularly the killing. I was much the youngest, perhaps that made it easier. I think Mother was forty-five or -six when I was born. She'd had two other children. My two brothers were grown up by the time I was ten.

And school?

I was very close to my nanny, I remember the horror when she left. I quite liked my prep school at Rottingdean. I was good at work and games and drew precociously. Someone showed me Rembrandt: I loved him. Like my father I went to Marlborough. It must have been 1928 or 1929. I wasn't popular. I was beaten a lot. A contemporary, a nice one, was Dickie Buckle. I painted and drew and won a drawing prize . . . I remember acting in school plays. I was Portia in Julius Caesar. I passed School Certificate at sixteen and wanted to leave; I wanted to do art. My brother John encouraged me. He must have been in his late twenties then. It was extraordinary and marvellous that he was able to persuade my parents to let me leave and pursue a career as an artist as young as sixteen.

So your brother played a big part in your life?

Both my brothers. John, my middle one, was artistic. He became a → 53

The monastery of Hilandar, Mount Athos, painted 1985–6 from drawings and colour notes done on the spot.

The Monastery of Hilandar, 1986 *oil on canvas 30 × 30 ins*
THE ARTIST

49

Painted near the Loire in 1939 within a week or two of the outbreak of war. Perhaps my best pre-war landscape.

Farm at Hussault on the Loire, 1939 *oil on canvas* *16 × 23 ins*
PRIVATELY OWNED

Between the Villino Corbignano and Settignano, this small hamlet inspired me by its Poussinesque architectural design. Painted on a misty morning when small, wild tulips covered the nearby fields.

Tuscan landscape below Settignano, c. 1950 *oil on canvas* *20 × 24 ins*
JOHN SWIRE

51

The stream Mensola and the little bridge over it which led from the road from Ponte a Mensola up to the Berenson's Villino Corbignano, where I stayed. An olive picker seated beneath the cyprus tree.

Bridge over the Mensola, c. 1950   *oil on cardboard*   *10 × 8 ins*
MARY COUNTESS OF PEMBROKE

The turn of the Arno, where I often went to paint when living at Berenson's Villino Corbignano in the early fifties.

The turn of the Arno, 1950   *oil on cardboard*   *10 × 12 ins*
MARY COUNTESS OF PEMBROKE

well-known interior decorator. He married and his children were gifted and they married gifted people. My niece by marriage, Caroline Hill, died sadly. She was a marvellous painter, or would have become one.

I remember a good male nude and the portrait of Graham Greene.

It is a brilliant portrait, really brilliant: in watercolour, which is very difficult to work in, for portraits. And my other niece by marriage, Selina, is making a name as a poet; her husband, Roderic, is a painter and so is my great nephew Inigo. My older brother was a businessman. He always looked after my money, about which I know nothing. So my family has been a marvellous support to me and I think of myself very much as a family person.

Yet you never married.

No. I could have married three times in my life and I did think about it. Once with an Italian girl, once with the artist, Mary Kessell, and then with a girl in Ireland.

Would marriage have suited you?

The Irish girl would have suited me, I think. Yes, I would have enjoyed marrying her. But the other two . . . no, it would have been really fatal, we wouldn't have got on. Mary I adored, but she was completely incapable of keeping a house or cooking, except for putting a baked potato in the oven –

Yes, unlike your housekeeper, Gracie.

Yes, unlike Gracie. Gracie's retired now but I always go and stay with her in her house; we spend Christmas together. The things that mean most to me are painting and travel. And neither is very well suited to

Grey Gowrie's brother at home in Donegal. I tried to show the angular uncertainty of youth. Malise has now become a well-known author.

The Hon. Malise Hore-Ruthven, 1959 *oil on canvas*   29 × 19 *ins*
MAJOR AND MRS DEREK COOPER

marriage. They are things you do by yourself. So I think I would have regretted getting married in the end. I've simply the wrong temperament and to have married would have violated part of my nature. You can't ask for everything. I've been lucky in so many ways. I don't resent or regret it really. I don't think very much about it.

So you left school early and started travelling early.

Yes. I went to Munich to study stage design. It was the period of great influence of the Bauhaus. And Schwitters came and talked to us.

You've never done abstracts or geometrical constructions or collages: you're not at all the kind of painter people would associate with the Bauhaus.

In Munich I did endless geometrical exercises including collages and my best landscapes have a completely abstract geometrical drawing underneath them. The geometrical underlining of any picture, the construction, has always been tremendously important to me. Later, I tried to apply my Bauhaus lessons to classical structures, the Golden Section for instance. My friendship with Victor Pasmore and his influence were a great help here.

And stage design?

In a way that was a false start though I did it for a long time and was quite successful at it. I studied and worked at stage design in Paris and Vienna after Munich. At nineteen I was taken up and fêted rather by what used to be called *haute Bohème*: people like Gerald Berners, Daisy Fellowes, Robert Irving and Barbara Ward. I worked in Paris with Paul Colin. Tilly Losch suggested I went to Vienna. I studied with Dr Josef Gregor, the librettist of Richard Strauss. It wasn't all study: I did the sets and costumes for Rameau's *Castor and Pollux* for the Oxford University Club and with Gregor I did the *Agamemnon* at the Burg

Theatre in Vienna. The Nazi occupation put an end to that production. Stage design launched me, gave me a name, brought me, I suppose, into an interesting society, very different from the one I knew. It gave my travels a purpose, though looking back I think that what I got out of travelling went much deeper than my work for the stage. You need a little praise at the start of your career. My sets and costumes for Freddie Ashton's ballet *The Lord of Burleigh* at Sadler's Wells went down well. An exhibition of them was introduced by Oliver Messel and Syrie Maugham gave me a party: all heady stuff to someone barely twenty.

But a false start?

Well, bit by bit it became clear to me that drawing and painting were the thing for me, that I admired painters more than designers. And then there was the interruption of the war, where stage work was concerned. I did go on . . . I did one thing, the sets and costumes for *Il Trovatore* at Covent Garden, just after the war. It wasn't a success. I shouldn't have done it. My father begged me not to: he said it was all too big for my first job of real importance, but I was insistent. He was right. I really regretted it; it wasn't good, I admit.

Do you perhaps give things up if they don't go wonderfully well?

I don't think it was that, because I was already much more involved in painting than in design by the time of the Covent Garden production. So I don't think it was that, though perhaps it was a bit. In theory I'd still like to do something for theatre again, for opera, before I die . . . The trouble is, I'm not a very theatrically-minded person. I'm a placid character in some respects at least and first-night hysterics or sopranos objecting to a dress I've designed and wanting to be made to look thinner – I'm not good at coping with all that. But in youth I certainly got a lot out of stage design. I had a fascinating six months in Moscow because of it. I was about nineteen. I worked with Tairov who ran the

The first sketch I did, on eighteenth-century canvas given me by Dr James White, then director of Ireland's National Gallery, of Tony O'Reilly, the famous Irish rugby player, now President of Heinz. He was wearing his 'rugger' jersey round his neck.

Tony O'Reilly, 1983 *oil on canvas* 16 × 14 ins THE ARTIST

Marcus McCausland painted in my Donegal studio shortly before his murder outside Londonderry.

Marcus McCausland, c. 1968 *oil on canvas* 18 × 18 ins MRS PETER WELSH

Kamerny theatre, and with Meyerhold. And I loved the performances: I went to more than sixty performances of theatre and ballet in Moscow, Kiev and Leningrad. I lived in the Hotel Novo Moscovskaya opposite St Basil's. The allowance my father gave me went a long way, then. I left Moscow and journeyed East; I remember nine days in a train across Siberia to Vladivostok. Then I went to Japan where I was an object of some fascination as there were few tourists there at that time. I was interviewed by the papers as 'A Tourist', a phenomenon. I stayed in the Frank Lloyd Wright Hotel. I loved the No Theatre and the Kabuki theatre and the puppet theatre at Osaka. I went to China, to Peking. I had a spell on a boat, as a steward, and later on I hitch-hiked to Ankor from Saigon. I loved Bali and its dancers: I must have lived for about six weeks with a Balinese family in the mountains.

Were you working at all during these travels?

Yes. I was drawing, looking and drawing.

Hitler's Munich, Stalin's Russia, Japan and China just before their war in 1937 . . . were you political at all, in the way of thirties intellectuals, or young people everywhere?

No. There was this intense military atmosphere and I loathed anything military. I'd seen the First World War film *All Quiet on the Western Front* when I was twelve: it made an immense impression. Of course we, all the theatre people and the painters, were fiercely anti-Nazi. The Nazis turned lots of the people I associated with into communists. I was in no sense a communist, ever, but I saw some things to admire in Russia. One was aware of the restrictions of life but not, in my case, of the terror. It was clear that conditions for ordinary people had improved a bit. The atmosphere was very puritan: tourists were taken to places called 'prophylactoriums', which were for the redemption of prostitutes, and our guides seemed inordinately proud of them. Perhaps →72

John Mangan, a local friend in Donegal, crippled since youth when he caught meningitis. When I painted him outside his whitewashed thatched cottage he had a home-made wheelchair and his dog was muzzled by a Heinz bean tin. Now John has a pretty wife and three splendid children.

John Mangan, 1961   *oil on canvas*   47½ × 59 *ins*
SIR HUGH LANE MUNICIPAL GALLERY OF MODERN ART, DUBLIN

58

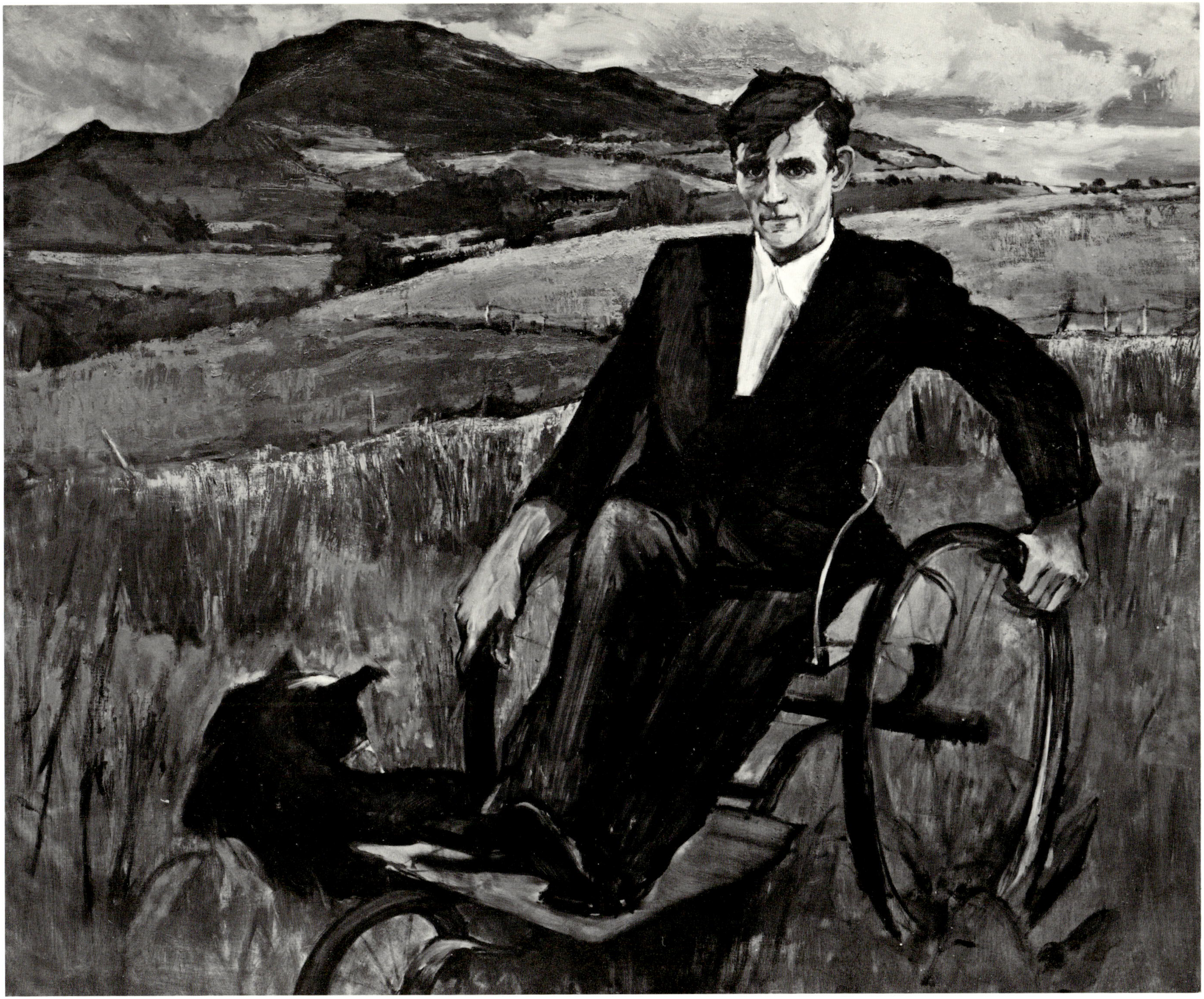

Sir John Heygate, who wrote *Decent Fellows*, a novel about Eton, during my youth. It caused such a scandal that it ruined John's life. Any grandmother could now read it without a blush. John was an ardent collector of modern works of art and a William Scott canvas is behind his head in this portrait.

Sir John Heygate, c. 1966 *oil on canvas* 18 × 16 ins RICHARD HEYGATE

Sir Hew Hamilton-Dalrymple, owner of the Bass Rock, still lives opposite that noble gannet-infested 'pile'. Another of my favourite portrait heads.

Sir Hew Hamilton-Dalrymple, Bt, c. 1968 *oil on canvas* 18 × 18 ins
SIR HEW HAMILTON-DALRYMPLE, BT

A landscape painted from the railway line near Orvieto.

opposite, top
Landscape near Orvieto, c. 1951 *oil on canvas* 9 × 16 ins THE ARTIST

The Girone (turn) of the Arno with Galileo's tower above Florence in the distance.

opposite, bottom
The Arno in January, c. 1951 *oil on panel* 5¾ × 11 ins MRS DUDLEY TOOTH

60

61

Hoeing the vines in the olive grove below the Villino Corbignano.
Hoeing the vines, 1950 *oil on canvas* 21 × 13½ *ins* DAVID M. WHITE

The downs at Long Crichel in Dorset on a hot summer afternoon looking towards Mrs Andrews' cottage.

Downs at Long Crichel, 1985 *oil on canvas* *15 × 30 ins* THE ARTIST

Painted in Florence in the early fifties. Igor Markevitch was the conductor at the Teatro Communale so the picture was called 'Markevitch concert – the last violin'.

Markevitch concert – the last violin, c. 1951   *oil on board*   *18 × 10 ins*
THE ARTIST

Alan Pryce-Jones, a friend since Vienna days in 1935 and 1936, when I studied there. His brilliant novel *The Pink Danube*, written under the pseudonym Arthur Pomphrey, caught all the nuances of that period.

opposite
Alan Pryce-Jones, c. 1980   *oil on canvas*   *18 × 18 ins*   ALAN PRYCE-JONES

I painted the Lord Chancellor, Lord Hailsham, in his House of Lords office, at his request without a wig.

over, left
The Viscount Hailsham, 1982   *oil on canvas*   *35 × 31½ ins*
THE PROVOST AND FELLOWS OF ETON COLLEGE

Sheridan Marquess of Dufferin and Ava painted at his home at Clandeboye in Northern Ireland, when he offered himself as model to the week's classes I gave there at a seminar organized by his wife Lindy. Another of my favourite and best-likeness male heads.

over, right
Sheridan Marquess of Dufferin and Ava, c. 1983
oil on canvas   *18 × 18 ins*   THE ARTIST

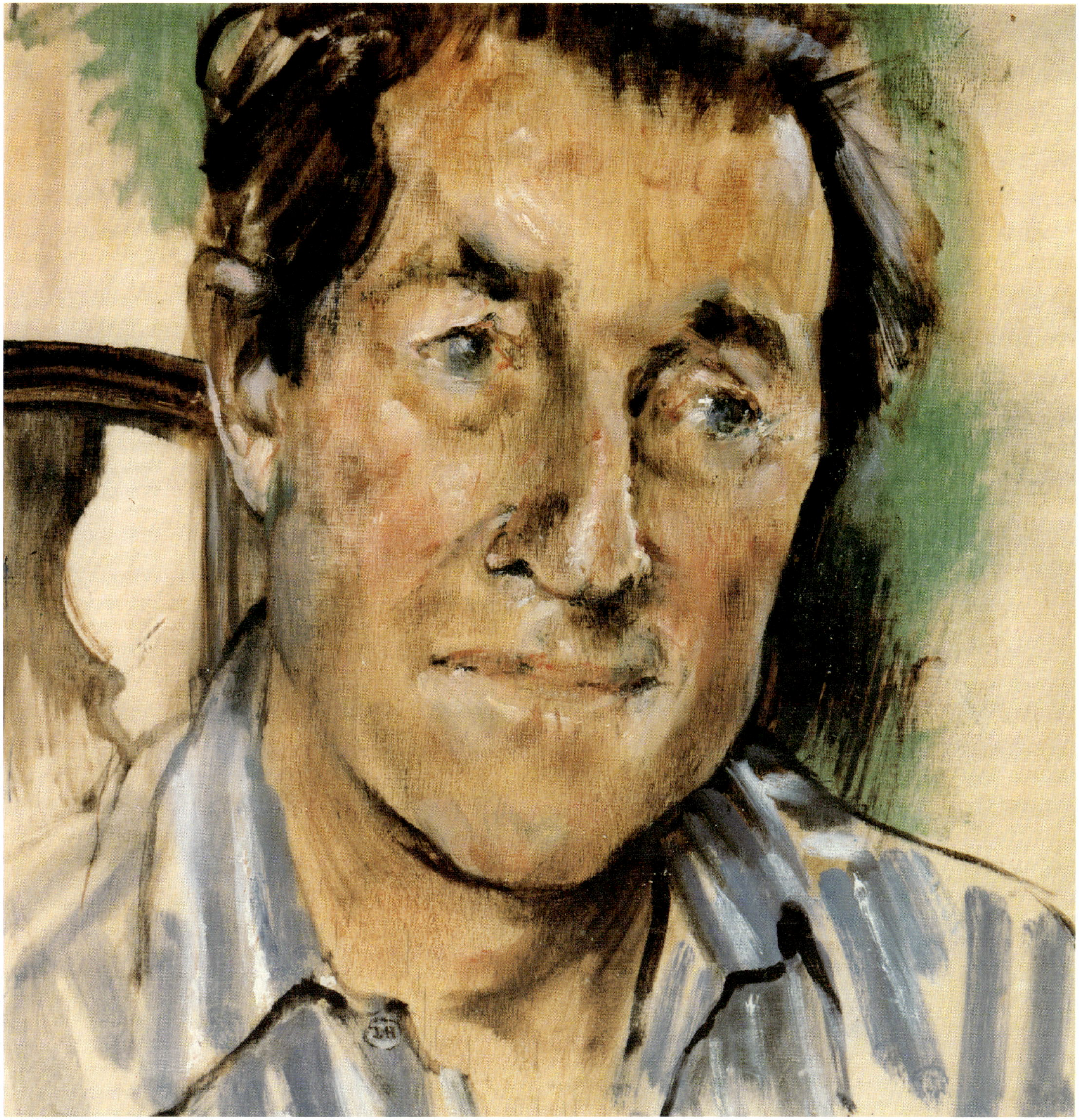

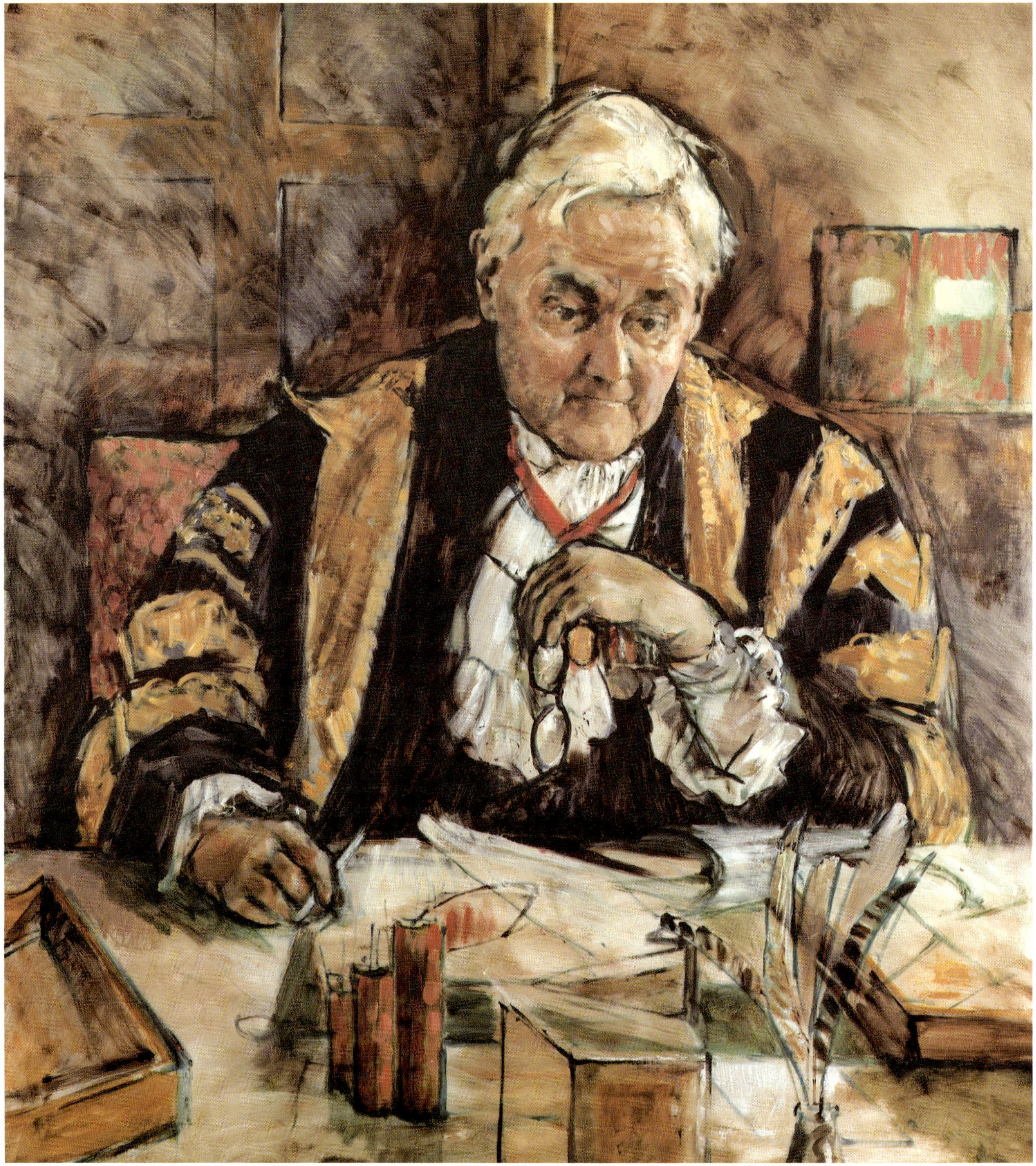

67

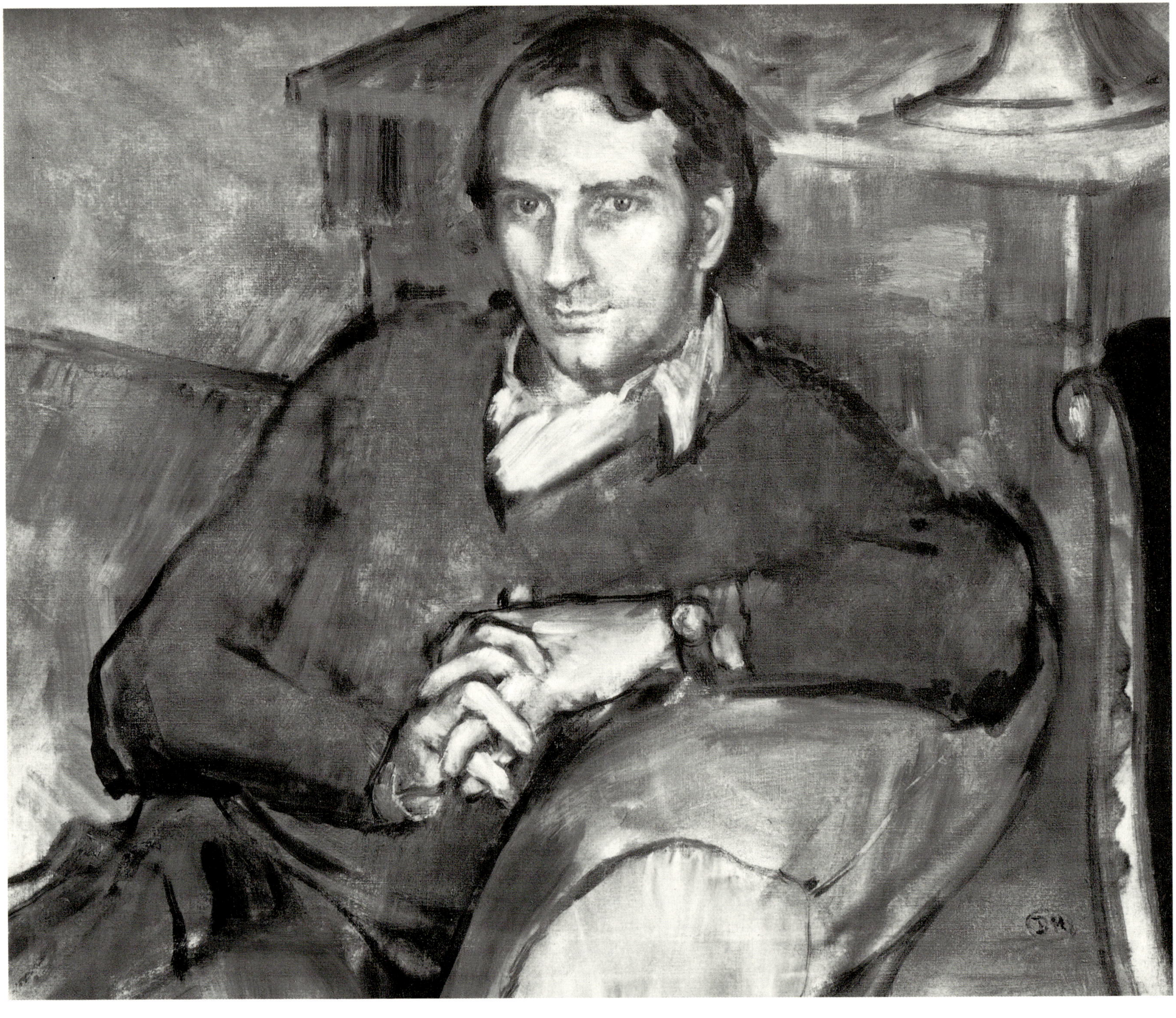

James Stafford — the young and brilliant Irish financier — also a collector of Renaissance bronzes and a wide selection of pictures.

James Stafford, 1977 *oil on canvas* 24 × 28 *ins* JAMES STAFFORD

A much-loved clerical figure in Donegal, Leslie Forrest has now become a canon in the Church of Ireland.

Leslie Forrest, 1981 *oil on canvas* 16 × 16 *ins*
THE REV. CANON LESLIE D. A. FORREST

Mariga Guinness, a German-born princess with a warm heart and infectious sense of enjoyment, who did so much for the Irish Georgian Society. She brought a trunk of dressing-up garments for me to choose from.

Mariga Guinness, 1967 *oil on canvas* 22 × 20 *ins*
THE HON. MRS MARIGA GUINNESS

I wanted to paint Lord Mountbatten, whom I had known as a child from Romsey days, as a human being and not as a national figurehead. So I told him if medals were needed they could be pinned on afterwards. I chose a fisherman's jersey – as he would have worn in Donegal where I saw him most, and as he was wearing only two days before his death on my last visit to him.

Lord Mountbatten, c. 1970 *oil on canvas* 18 × 18 ins
COUNTESS MOUNTBATTEN OF BURMA

Sacha Abercorn, the scholar of the family and a Jung disciple, descended from the Tsar's family as well as from Pushkin.

The Marchioness of Hamilton, 1976 *oil on canvas* 16⅞ × 17¼ ins
THE DUCHESS OF ABERCORN

A dedicated humanist and help to those in trouble, head of a brilliant literary family.

opposite
The Earl of Longford, 1977 *oil on canvas* 24 × 20 ins
THE HON. THOMAS PACKENHAM

71

John Bryson, a friend over many years, an Oxford don at Balliol and collector of drawings, bronzes and other works of art. He was Grey Gowrie's tutor. I feel this picture to be among my best heads.

John Bryson, c. 1964   *oil on canvas*   21¾ × 15⅝ ins
MRS EDWIN BRYSON

Dr Leland Lyons, the late Provost of Trinity College, Dublin. Painted in the beautiful hall of the Provost's Lodge. A brilliant historian and a very considerate sitter.
over, left
Dr Leland Lyons, 1980   *oil on canvas*   30 × 28 ins
TRINITY COLLEGE, DUBLIN

John Betjeman was at Marlborough with my brother John and was also a lifelong friend. When at Marlborough myself I was given *Mount Zion*, his first book of poems, and he later gave me his other works, all with amusing dedications and often signed Sean McBetjeman. He loved Ireland and came there to be painted. In our spare time we gathered mussels.
over, right
Sir John Betjeman, 1975   *oil on canvas*   18 × 18 ins
JOHN MURRAY LTD

72

I should have been more political, but I wasn't.

And in the war you were a pacifist, a conscientious objector?

Yes. I registered. I wouldn't fight. I did war work, of course, as you rightly had to. The thing that perhaps made me into a pacifist was one of my first memories. We lived near the main road from Winchester to Southampton. There was a little wood where soldiers came to collect their horses before they were shipped off to France: remount camps I think they were called. It must have been near the end of the First War. I remember it quite well.

The wounds?

No, not wounds, but all day long we heard soldiers marching down to the ships, and the noise of the horses' hooves. Somehow or other I knew my mother thought they would never come back.

Did your father fight?

No, he would have been too old. I think he was a Territorial or something.

And your war work?

I worked on farms. I can't say I liked it much, milking at four in the morning in order to catch the milk train and de-magotting sheep. I liked anti-aircraft duty better.

Derek, your portraits – many, perhaps most, of them are of people with a lot of prestige in our society, what used to be called the Establishment. Haven't you found them rather resentful of your pacifism? They're usually pretty fierce about consciencious objectors.

→ 82

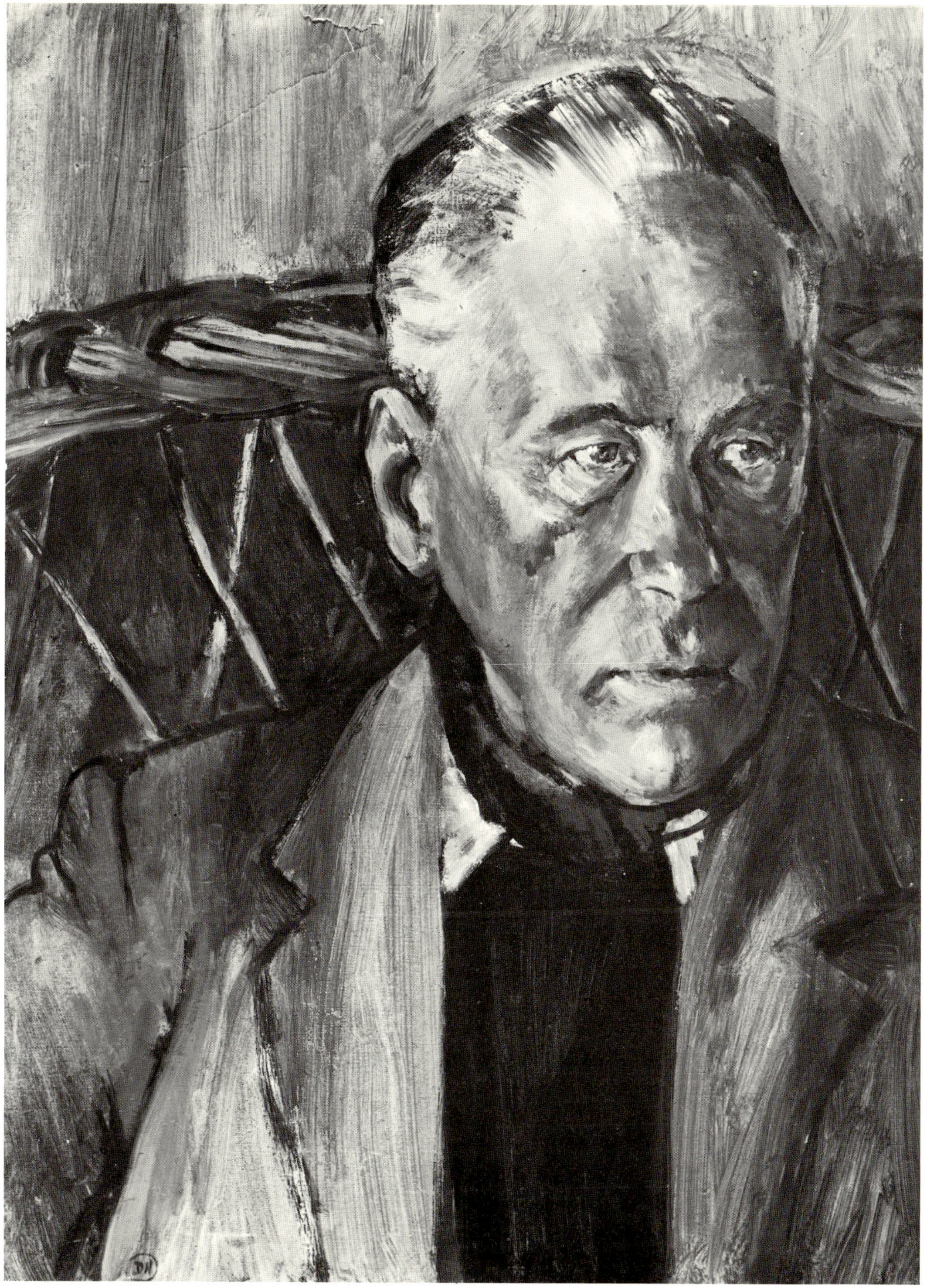

74

75

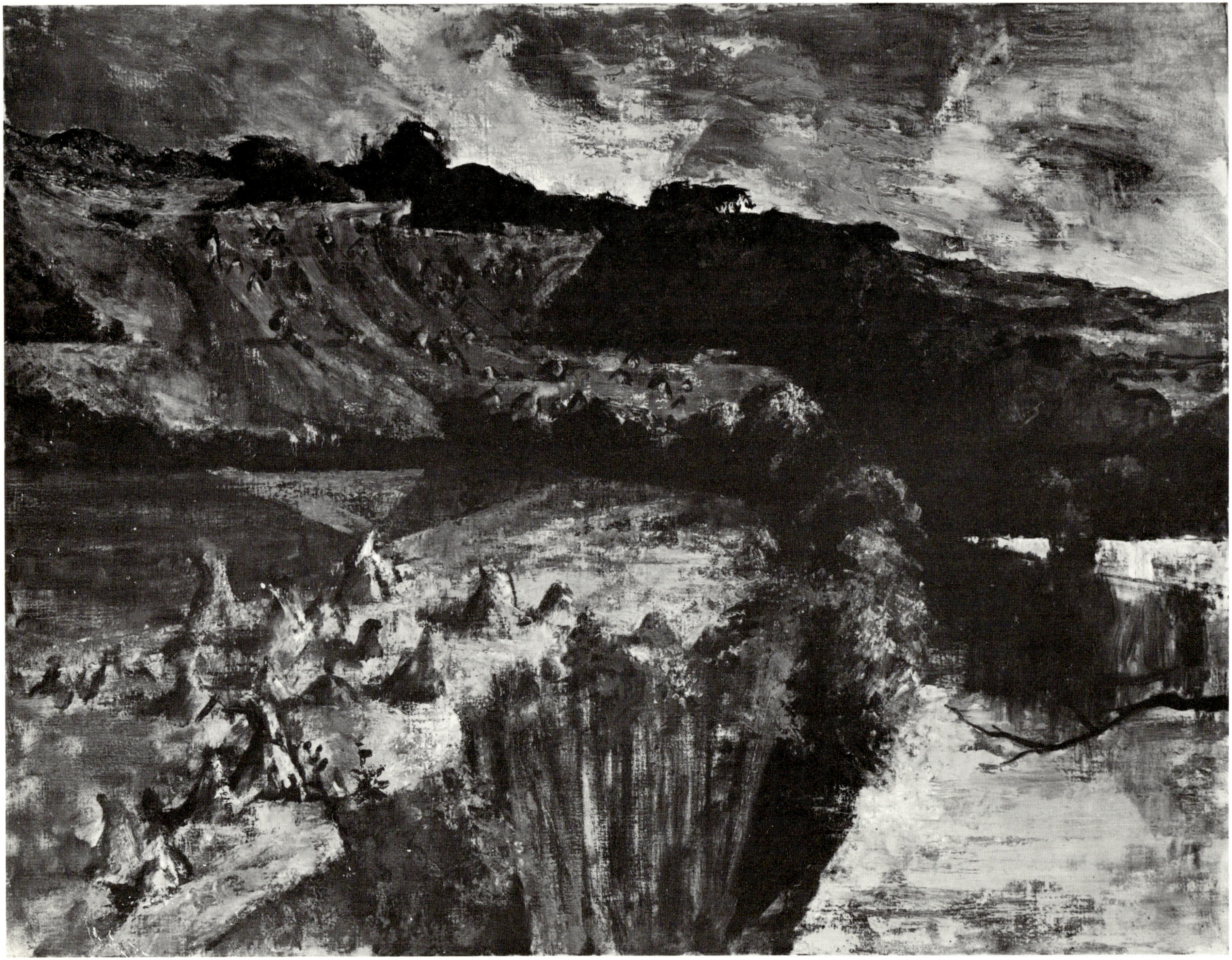

A small picture of a distant view from my Tory Island hut of a cow grazing near the sea.

Cow grazing on Tory Island, 1982   *oil on board*   *8 × 10 ins*
THE ARTIST

A BBC film about me and my paintings opened by showing this picture and the bridge from which it was painted – probably the most geometric picture I ever did. I made a completely abstract drawing of its construction, then clothed the bare bones with the landscape in front of me.

Donegal late harvest, *c.* 1962   *oil on canvas*   *36 × 48 ins*
GLEBE GALLERY, CHURCHILL, CO. DONEGAL

Tory Island. The great seaward-straining cliffs seen in a stormy afternoon light from my hut. In the far distance Fanad Head on the mainland.

View from my hut on Tory Island, 1981　*oil on canvas*　7 × 16 *ins*　THE ARTIST

Midnight from my Tory hut. The 'round tower' moonlit in the middle distance.

Midnight from my Tory hut, 1980 *oil on cardboard*   8 × 12 ins   THE ARTIST

Painted from the loo seat at Classiebawn Castle with Ben Bulben (Yeats' mountain) seen across Donegal Bay. This was when Lord Mountbatten lent me the castle, my being unable to reach Tory Island because of the violent gales.

Ben Bulben from Classiebawn, c. 1968 *oil on board*   7 × 10 ins   THE ARTIST

Another view towards the east from my Tory Island hut.

View towards the east from my Tory hut, 1978 *oil on canvas* 7 × 18 ins
LORD O'NEILL

'The Season of Thaw' – painted from the old Post Office in Churchill Village where I live. This picture won a Contemporary Art Society prize and was hung at the Tate Gallery before the Herbert Gallery in Coventry acquired it.

The Season of Thaw, 1956 *oil on canvas* 20 × 35½ ins
THE HERBERT GALLERY, COVENTRY

No, on the whole I haven't. My army friends were especially understanding and unpunishing.

Lord Mountbatten, for instance?

No, he never took it out on me, he wouldn't. I knew the first airborne soldiers who landed in France after D-Day. They came to supper on the farm about two nights before they left for France and some were killed. I didn't know they were going, but I suspected it. They were all incredibly sympathetic and understanding about the pacifism.

But not everyone?

No. I worked on one farm where the old grandmother had taught her canary to whistle 'Land of Hope and Glory'. It must have been a very old canary, too, because I think she'd taught it the tune in the First War. She used to point at me during the worst moments of war horror, after the worst announcements on the wireless, and say, 'Now you listen to this. He's singing this for you.'

Do you regret not fighting, has that left a wound?

I can't regret it because I still feel very strongly about it. Violence is so sad and squalid: two people I've painted have been murdered. Of course it did leave a sort of chip on the shoulder: one felt one wasn't sharing in some great catastrophe, or great historical moment. I had a friend, a paratrooper, and, as I said, I suspected that he and his friends were going off into deadly danger. I nearly gave in then one night and thought, 'I can't keep this up any more, I must join in myself.' But I didn't.

You knew Keith Vaughan at that time, he was also a CO. He did remarkable drawings and paintings during the war.

A gloomy scene showing the dour side of Tory Island. Harsh stone wall, glowering skies and rain-soaked hayricks.
Tory Island hayricks, 1960   *oil on canvas*   29 × 26 ins   DAVID CLARKE

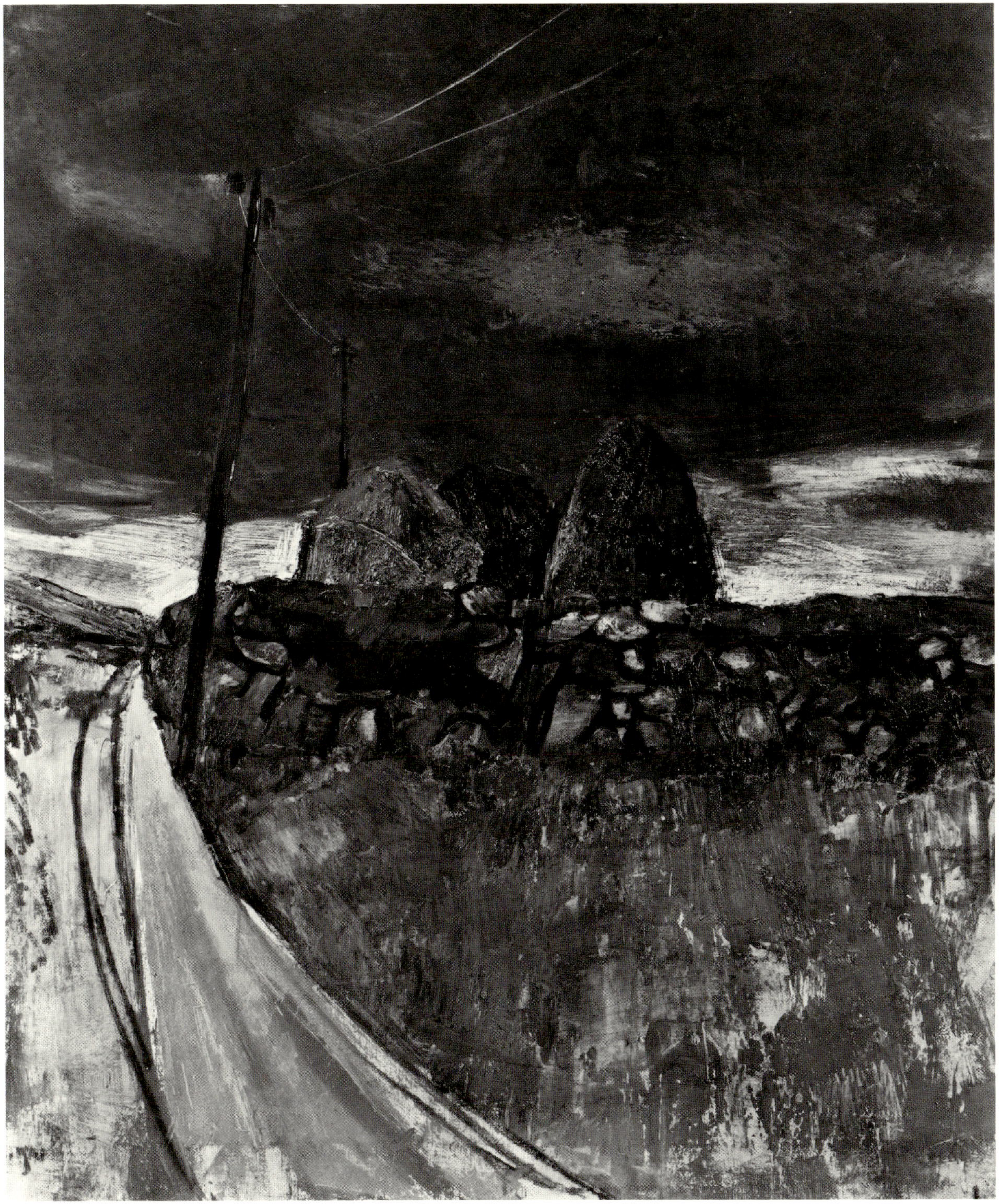

He did, yes, wonderful work. I hardly did anything during the war, very little that was worthwhile.

Yet you knew you were going to be a painter?

From the end of the war I painted seriously, without stopping for any length of time. The commitment really started before the war; the war got in the way of everyone's life. I'd had a studio in Paris in 1938 and I also rented an old mill on the Loire and painted landscapes there. I was encouraged by Edward Molyneux. He really set me on my way. He was a remarkable man, a London newspaper boy who became one of the greatest couturiers in Paris, one of the greatest of all time. His clothes made him a fortune and he became one of the great art collectors of the century. His first collection was eighteenth-century French drawings, Watteau and Hubert Robert and so on. He sold these, or many of them, to Lady Mendl and then he started buying the Impressionists. He bought Manet and Monet but also Corot and Van Gogh. I knew him because he saw one painting of mine, a head, and he arrived at my studio and said, 'Forgive me bursting in but you must paint. Give up stage design. I shall arrange for my car to call for you every day after I've been dropped at the office and take you to look at everything you want to see in Paris. And then you must paint and in the evenings I'll have you collected again and you can compare what you've done with the paintings in my collection.' So I was able to study great Impressionist painting at leisure, in his apartment on the Quai d'Orsay. After the war he sold the collection to Mrs Ailsa Mellon Bruce and they're now the basis of the National Gallery in Washington's Impressionist collection. So you see they were very great examples. In the 1950s Mrs Bruce bought four of my small Donegal pictures and I was able to tell her that it was because of her collection that I became a painter.

You did in fact exhibit some of your first paintings in the war?

West End Village scene on Tory, a burst of sunlight between heavy rain.

Fields behind West Town, 1962 *oil on canvas* *31 × 46 ins*
ANDREW HEGARTY

I was in a group show at Reid and Lefèvre early on; Sir Edward Marsh bought a work, I remember. I had my first one-man show at the Nicholson gallery in the middle of the war. But as I've said, it seemed like a sterile period to me. I only really felt like a painter after the war was over.

Had that anything to do with Ireland?

Yes, a lot. I didn't go to live there, of course, until later, until the middle fifties. But right after the war I travelled and painted in the west of Ireland, on Achill Island particularly. It made a tremendous impression. I stayed in a little bungalow, a cottage right on the beach, with the pounding waves and the gigantic cliffs so near. It was visual, it wasn't a Celtic Revival sort of thing: I wasn't painting Synge's *Riders to the Sea*. The work was romantic because the place felt romantic, and perhaps I was influenced by the romantic revival going on in English painting, by Sutherland in particular —

Not an idiom, I feel, that suits you.

No, I agree. But it was part of me at the time; I saw things dramatically, as if through Sutherland's eyes. I knew him and liked him immensely and I have a lot of his pictures: the best ones I think, the Pembroke paintings. But it wasn't the right idiom for me, except that it forced me to focus on landscape, my preferred subject as a painter. I had to learn that what was right for me was a much more classical, and more geometric – in that sense a more modern – approach. There was the effect of the Bauhaus training which I've mentioned and in the war I made friends with Victor Pasmore and Lawrence Gowing. Pasmore influenced me a good deal, but it took time. I bought his work, and Gowing's. Lawrence was a marvellous painter and for me that was his best period, the forties, the apple pictures and the landscapes done in Wiltshire, near where I was doing farm work. Some of Victor's great

Painted on a Sunday afternoon and the following day from the top of
the 'anvil' on Tor More. The whole island spread out below.

Tory Island from Tor More, 1958 *oil on canvas* *28 × 48 ins*
THE ULSTER MUSEUM, BELFAST

pictures of the Thames and Hammersmith were done in the war and the one I have, the misty London landscape, must have been done in the late forties. Victor confirmed a respect for proportion and the geometrical underlay of painting: I start by looking at a view and then I make a geometric drawing out of it.

On the board or canvas?

No, on paper or a scrap of anything to hand, and then I work freely on the board or canvas.

So you apply paint without charcoal or pencil?

I seldom use charcoal or pencil. I mean I may have at the beginning, in the forties, divided up the canvas that way into various sections to get proportion and harmony, but as things went on I'd do the landscape freely so you could see it emerge from the paint.

And you used to talk to Pasmore about painting?

Yes, a lot. He, of course, has his colour system, his notation: I mean, if he uses a particular red he knows exactly what other colours at different points in the spectrum will work with it. I've always admired him as a painter and I thought the furious row that went with his shift to abstraction was altogether irrelevant. I've got a version of the *Isles of Greece*, that beautiful picture in the Tate, and another of the same period. They are the first rather maze-like abstracts that suggest, perhaps, the landscape drawings of Van Gogh . . . I feel the least satisfactory phase in his career was when he started to make constructions. They didn't inspire me. But he is a great man.

You said that what was right for you was a more classical approach. Italy and Italian painting are important in your life and work, are they not? → 98

A small sunset from my hut.

Sunset from my hut, 1970 *oil on canvas* 4 × 5 ins THE ARTIST

Where HMS *Wasp* sank in 1884. A boat sent to collect tax from Tory Island sank at this point with only a few lives saved.

Where the Wasp sank, 1978 *oil on wood* 4 × 8 ins HRH THE PRINCE OF WALES

The other side of Donegal. A serene afternoon looking from fields near Moville towards Benevena and Limavady; across Lough Foyle to Northern Ireland and the east.

Towards Benevena from Moville, 1982   *oil on canvas*   *7 × 16 ins*
NOËL ATCHESON

One of my favourite parts of Ireland – the Burren in County Clare. A strange, grey, almost Max-Ernst moonscape scene with lush green valleys below the limestone hills and the well-known and beautiful wild flowers growing among the rock cleavages. Strangely enough a very rarely painted area of Ireland.

The Burren in County Clare, *c.* 1978   *oil on canvas* *8 × 18 ins*
THE ARTIST

Another small 'square' picture done in Denmark when painting a portrait of the Lord Chamberlain, Mr Morten, now in the Danish National Portrait Gallery. A hot thundery day.

Thunder in Denmark, c. 1976   *oil on board*   10 × 10 *ins*
THE ARTIST

Towards Tory Island lighthouse – afternoon light from my hut 'verandah'.

Tory Island lighthouse from my 'verandah', c. 1968   *oil on canvas*
10 × 10 *ins*   THE ARTIST

From the crag above Balcarres in Fife one can look across to Berwick Law and the Lammermoors behind. An early spring day with snow still on the distant hills.

The Lammermoors under snow from Balcarres, *c.* 1968   *oil on canvas*
10 × 10 ins   THE HON. THOMAS LINDSAY

Painted near Menerbes in France – the view from a window with a Chinese vase on the windowsill.

Vase in a window near Menerbes, 1984   *oil on wood*   *5 × 4 ins*
HM QUEEN ELIZABETH THE QUEEN MOTHER

Taken from the Rublev Trinity, painted during the war and posed by three local figures in Wiltshire.

The Rublev Trinity, *c.* 1940   *oil on linen stretched over wood*   *12 × 8 ins*
MAJOR AND MRS DEREK COOPER

My bed in the Gothic bedroom at Schloss Vaduz in Liechtenstein. I always had this room when a guest there, painting landscapes and portraits as well.

Gothic bedroom, 1980   *oil on canvas*   *7 × 9 ins*   *THE ARTIST*

Dawyck Haig, himself an extremely good and serious artist, who started painting when prisoner at Colditz. A friend and pupil of Victor Pasmore. We've known each other since pre-war Austrian holidays and have often swapped pictures since then.

opposite
The Earl Haig, 1983   *oil on canvas*   *16 × 18 ins*   *THE EARL HAIG*

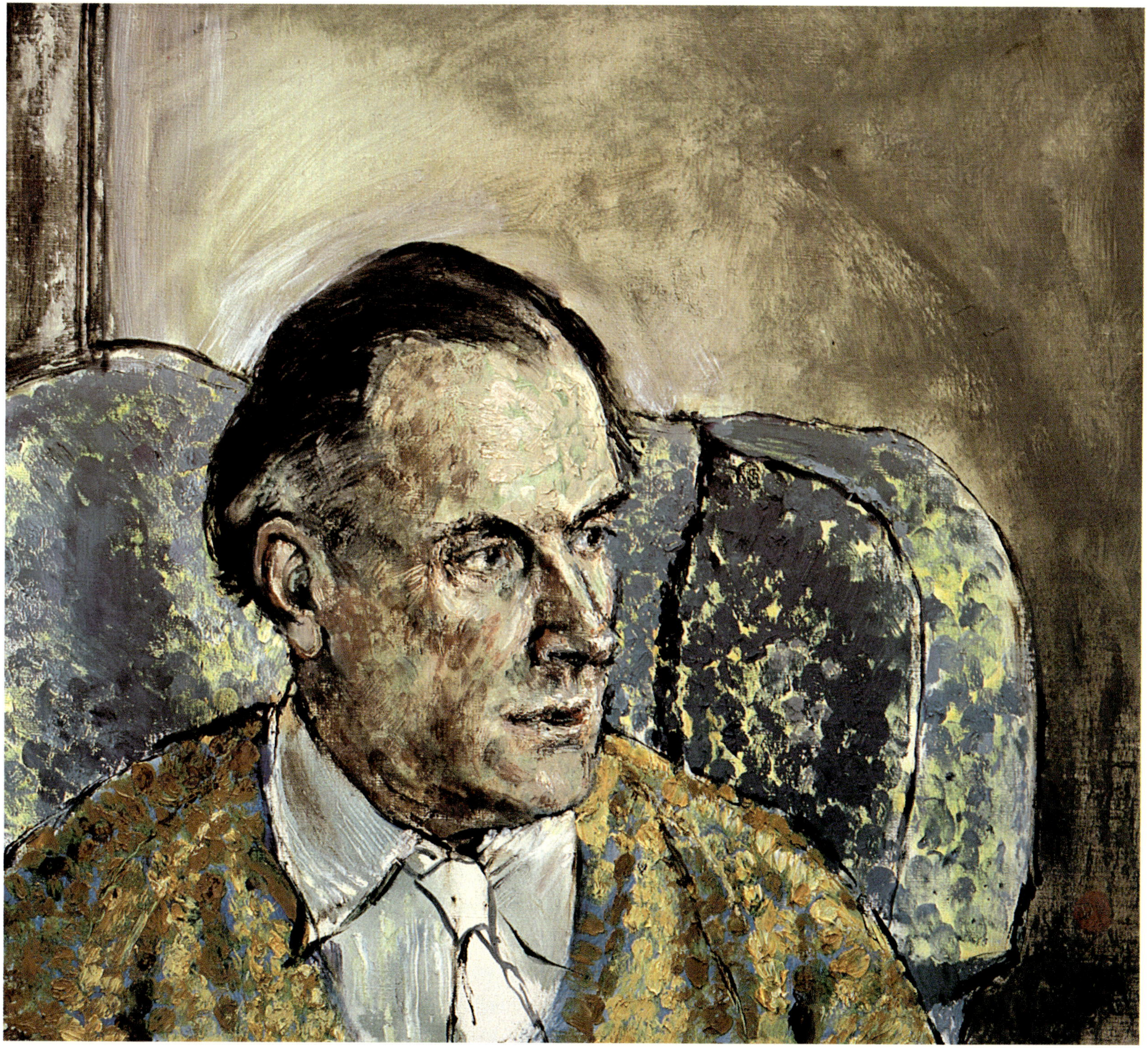

Raymond Mortimer, who once said the only fate he knew worse than death would be to be painted by me! He later relented and I did this small head of him in Venice.

Raymond Mortimer, 1975 *oil on wood* 7½ × 7½ *ins* PAUL HYSLOP

Prince Ludwig of Hesse whom I first knew when studying theatre design in Munich in the early thirties. A great lover of the arts, especially music, and with his Scottish wife patron of Benjamin Britten for many years.

His Royal Highness Prince Ludwig of Hesse, c. 1975 *oil on canvas* 16 × 16 *ins*
HRH PRINCESS MARGARET OF HESSE AND THE RHINE

Sligo hills seen from above Classiebawn Castle with a figure swiftly passing by in a cart.

Sligo hills from Classiebawn Castle, c. 1968 *oil on canvas 16 × 30 ins*
FORMERLY OWNED BY MRS GRISEWOLD

Oh immensely. More than anything, perhaps, except the physical experience of Ireland. Even with Corot, an obvious admiration, it's the Campagna pictures, the early classical ones which I like best. I first went to Italy when I was about eighteen, to Florence. In the fifties I was art director at the British School in Rome for nearly five years in all: I used to spend the winters there. I was a sort of nanny to young British painters who were out there on grants and scholarships. I'd take them on trips, up to the Veneto or down south or round the collections in Rome, as well as introducing them to Guttuso and other Italian artists. I gave a lot of parties because before I came to the school they used to sit around in the common room rather pathetically, hardly daring to go out. Most of them couldn't speak Italian and they didn't particularly like the food.

Whom are we talking about?

Oh, there was Henry Inlander, Derrick Greaves, Michael Andrews, John Bratby, Tony Fry, Joe Tilson.

You like Bratby's work very much, don't you?

Yes. It's uneven of late but I think he's a neglected painter.

His best painting, in my view, is the one you own. I put it in my essay on British painting, the person ill in bed —

It's his wife in bed with jaundice, painted in those Rome years. And I admire Mike Andrews enormously. He was homesick in Rome, I'm afraid, as he was very much involved with his own circle of friends in London who really constituted his subject-matter . . . but he did one of his best things in Rome, a picture of a girl on the Spanish Steps. And Derrick Greaves's work, the roofs of San Marco in Venice was painted at that time. Inlander was good too, he should get more attention.

One of my first winters at Churchill. Lake Gartan or Lough Veagh ('lough of the birches') dark and forbidding and the 'garden' seen from the house, St Columb's, not yet laid out.

Lake Gartan, 1958   *oil on canvas*   24 × 30 ins   DAVID CLARKE

Did you paint much in Rome yourself?

Well, I was rather taken up with the students and with lecturing during those Rome winters; I painted the rest of the year in Ireland. But I did paint in Italy before and after being at the school, as this book shows. It was a crucial experience for me. Contemporary French painters, Parisian painters, didn't inspire me like the Italians. And except for Rothko and Tobey, whom I admire, the Americans, who were starting to come into fashion at that time, meant rather little. I felt the Italians led the world then, painters like Vespignani and Guttuso and above all Morandi.

You knew Morandi?

Through a friend in the war. Before I met him, I'd heard that he couldn't get hold of English paints, which he used: Roberson's, the best in the world. Tragically, they've just closed down. I've used them myself for forty years. They came in blue oblong boxes, very distinctive, which used to feature in Morandi's still lifes. So I gave some to an army friend to take to him and somehow he succeeded, during the allied invasion of Italy. Then after the war I went to see him when I was living at Berenson's. He gave me a little flower painting and a landscape etching. I bought a watercolour. I'd visit him often. He lived with his two sisters. You got to his studio through their bedroom, which had bentwood beds. The studio windows were always veiled, covered with mutton cloth, muslin, to stop hard light creeping in. You know that wonderful sort of veiled light of his paintings? He painted slowly and intensely. I revered him. He is the most concentrated painter of our century and one of the absolute best. He lived like a monk and looked rather like one, with a slight fringe of hair and teeth like Byzantine ivories. It was a thoroughly bourgeois flat in Bologna and yet so odd, with the two sisters sharing the same room and the veiled studio beyond it. We corresponded off and on.

The year the field below St Columb's was sown with oats. A great crop. Unfortunately the weight of the binder caved in the turf drainage system and the field is now planted with groups of birches. A view taken from the front of the house. The very old alder in the field (centre) was blown down by Hurricane Debbie in 1962.

Harvesting at St Columb's, *c.* 1960   *oil on canvas*   26 × 30 *ins*
SIR ALFRED BEIT, BT

101

And did you like Afro?

Yes, but less than Zoran Music; I bought two fine Musics. I enjoyed my friendship with these painters, and got to know them in quite a concentrated way because, unlike England, or *haute Bohème*, there wasn't much social mixing in Italy. Painters and writers and intellectuals didn't mix with so-called Society all that much.

Did you find them agreeable?

Oh yes, agreeable, but they were terribly locked into their own little circle. They never made an effort to break the circle or get out of it. There were exceptions. There was Mimi Pecci Blunt, who would invite writers, painters and musicians. And Princess Caetani, who backed the marvellous literary magazine *Botteghe Oscure*, but she was American. The French or Polish painter, Balthus, was there. He was invited sometimes. His landscapes are staggeringly good.

And the obsessive pictures of adolescent girls?

I do like them, and they are also amusing in a sly, rather disquieting way. The Japanese-looking ones are masterpieces: ladies on the floor crawling towards a piece of furniture. And Alberto Burri was taken up a bit, as I remember.

Burri would be a surprising painter for you to like, all that sacking and charred wood and what look like French letters –

Oh I liked *him*, not the paintings, though they were skilful. He used to come to the school and I remember visiting his studio. He'd string up tins of baked beans or tomatoes and shoot at them with a rifle. And then the bullet-ridden and splattered tin would be mounted on a beautiful plinth of Cararra marble and he'd say, 'Oh, I'll get a thousand

The same view as the one done at midnight looking towards the Donegal mainland from my hut on Tory Island.

View from my hut on Tory Island, *c.* 1965 *oil on canvas* 8 × 12 *ins*
JAMES RUSSELL

After a heavy rain shower – the rocks white and glittering with water. The track to the lighthouse where I got my buckets of drinking-water seen on the left.

Towards the lighthouse after rain, 1980 *oil on cardboard* 8 × 10 *ins*
THE ARTIST

The first head I painted of Freddie Mills, the world welterweight champion boxer. I used to go to Solomons' Gym to draw boxers in action. I painted another portrait of Freddie later and also one of his wife. Freddie was a good and kind man – a gentleman in every sense. This picture once belonged to the now extinct British Gallery of Sporting Art.

Freddie Mills, *c.* 1950   *oil on canvas*   *10 × 18 ins*   THE ARTIST

pounds for that!' He'd let the students have a go, which thrilled them of course.

But the serious friendship of your Italian years was Berenson.

It was more than friendship. I was completely devoted to him and to Nicky Mariano, his companion. Both my parents died, you see, in the early fifties, when I was living part of the year with BB and Nicky. He lent me the little villa in the grounds of his great villa, I Tatti. They became my family.

What was Berenson's conversation like?

It was a serious place, there was quiet and work and reading but mealtimes could be dazzling with arguments in every European language taking place at the same time and somehow getting through. His talk could be an education, a life in itself; certainly it brought me into a life I'd never known.

Talk about painting?

Oh, it might be about painting, but not necessarily. By the time I knew him his instinct, his judgement for painting was still very fine but somehow he'd moved on, out of art and into life . . . he'd somehow got over the whole thing, not the looking but he'd moved away from the scholarship and the art dealing. The thing he really loved was nature, his garden. He'd moved on, in a way.

Away from art?

Not exactly. He was still writing. He wrote *Sketch for a Self-portrait*, which some people think is his best book, while I was there and I seem to remember an essay on Piero della Francesca and on Sienese painting.

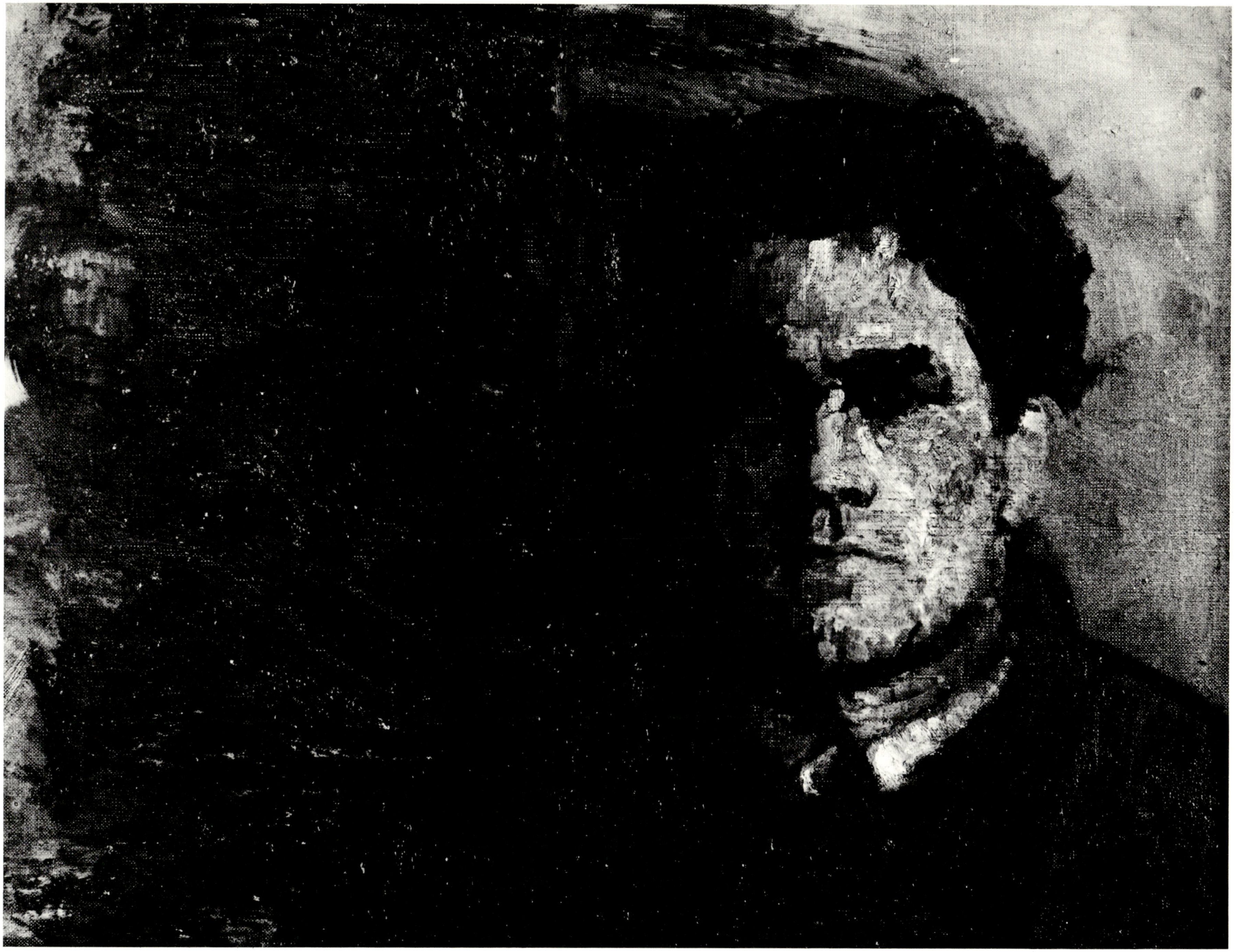

His criticisms of my painting were always apt. He had an infallible sense of the weak spot in any painting even if, as was often the case, one disagreed with his reasoning as to *why* it was weak.

Did he have much feeling for modern paintings?

Not in the sense most people would understand but nevertheless a profound feeling. He said that Picasso was the greatest draughtsman since Raphael, without question. He'd bought Matisse very early on. He thought very highly of John Berger as a critic: not the attacks on the bourgeoisie but as the only person in Europe who looked at paintings as if they were individuals, people.

What did he think of your paintings?

He liked the picture of himself and Nicky, of Nicky reading to him. I own it now because Nicky left it to me when she died. He liked the olive-pruner series, though not as much as Kenneth Clark did. He alas never saw my Irish paintings, as K. did. Like K., he liked my paintings enough to own a few because he wasn't sentimental about his acquisitions. He encouraged me in every way. He wrote the introduction to my first Islamic book.

Your paintings of Berenson bring us to portrait painting generally. I'd like to spend a bit of time talking about your best-known work, your portraits, before ending with what I believe to be your best work, your Irish landscapes. You weren't recognized, really, as a painter of well-known people until when, the late 1950s?

Not until after then, not until Bryan Robertson put on a retrospective show of my work at the Whitechapel Gallery in 1962. One or two portraits in that show attracted attention. The Berenson paintings, obviously; Mrs Waterfield, who had been painted by Watts as a girl.

Done from a drawing made at the Freddie Mills – Gus Lesnevitch fight at Harringay Stadium.

Harringay boxing match, 1948 *oil on canvas* 20 × 30 ins THE ARTIST

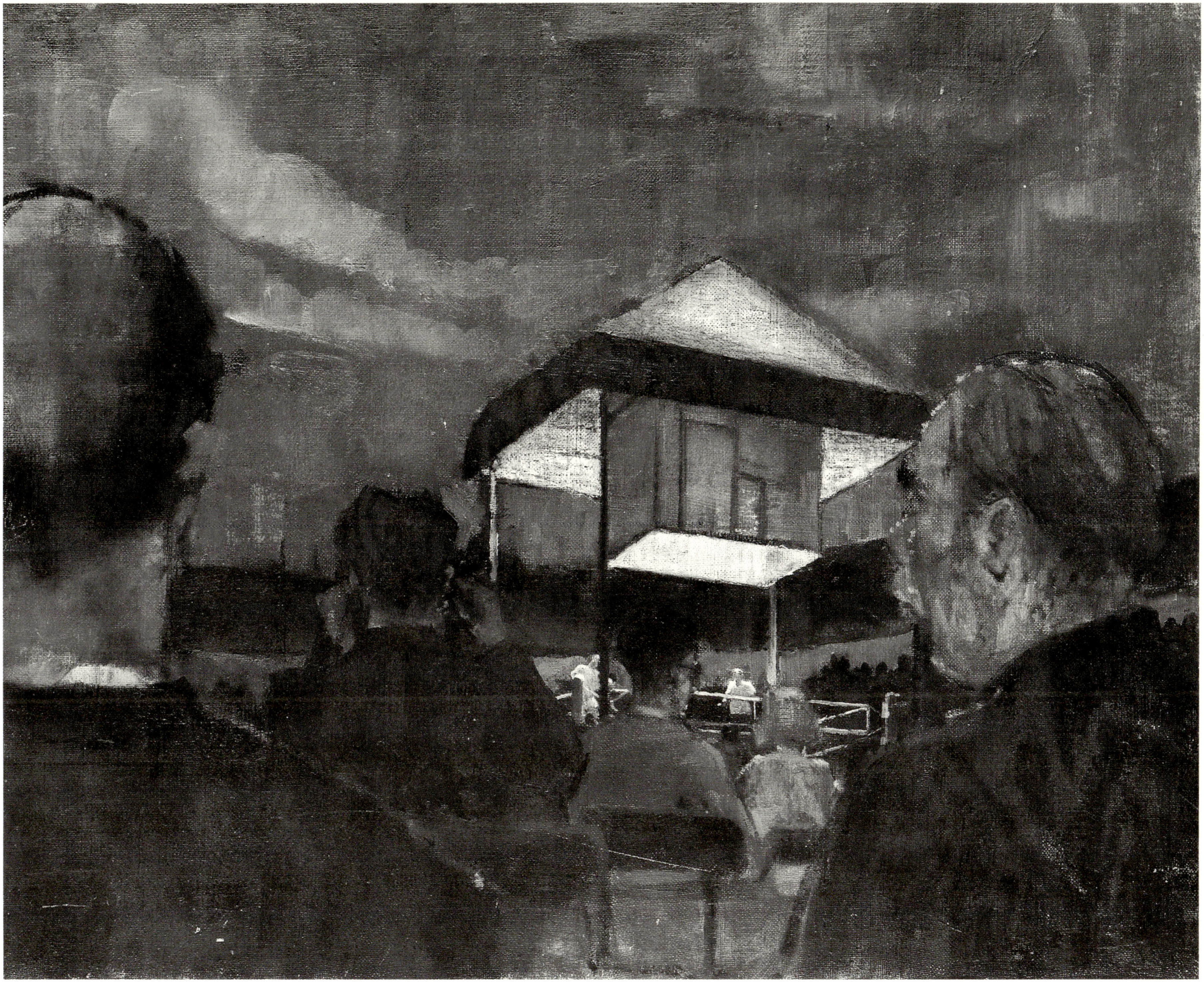

The Arts Council bought that one. The portrait of a seated young man, your brother in fact. Freddie Mills, the boxer. That portrait was noticed particularly by John Russell —

— *Who wrote the book on Francis Bacon?*

Yes. He said I painted him hard and soft, tough and soft like his boxing-glove. I painted Freddie because I'd done one or two other boxing pictures; I used to draw at that gymnasium in Windmill Street called Solomons' gym. It was difficult and challenging to draw boxers: the movement and the punching, the lurch after a punch. Freddie Mills and his wife became friends. I also did a portrait of Don Cockle.

So demand built up after the Whitechapel show. One side of your personality, and your life, is the man with a very wide social acquaintance and many friends. People would ask you to paint them?

Yes, or I would ask them. As I've said, I don't accept commissions in the formal sense. I do four or five portraits a year and there's no obligation for anyone to buy them. It's always a sensitive issue.

Sensitive on both sides, for painter and sitter?

Of course. I painted Freddie Ashton, at his request, though I was tremendously pleased to do so, years ago. He didn't like the picture. He said, 'Oh Derek, I thought you'd make me look beautiful.' So he didn't buy it. I'm pleased in a way, because it's now in the Tate. Freddie says he regrets it now because much more recently David Hockney did drawings of him and he says he's even less beautiful because now he's got a nose like raspberry jam. He's very funny about it. He's wonderful-looking anyway, with or without the raspberry nose.

You have a reputation for getting on well with your sitters. I remember that

Grace Dixon's window on Tory Island. Grace was the only sister of four brothers living on the island. Two brothers were the painters James Dixon and Johnny Dixon, both fishermen as well. Grace, the last Dixon on the island, was a great gardener and died at the age of ninety-nine.

Grace Dixon's window, 1978 *oil on wood*   11 × 10 *ins*   THE ARTIST

The President of the John Deere Company of Moline, Illinois: William Hewitt. He later became American ambassador to Jamaica. I painted him on a balcony of his beautiful Saarinen-designed factory but was told later he had cut out the architectural parts of the picture, on which its whole composition depended, leaving only himself. If so, it was hardly a diplomatic gesture and certainly one to hurt the artist! I hope it wasn't true.

William Hewitt, c. 1966   *oil on board*   *30 × 45 ins*   JOHN DEERE COMPANY

Sir Frederick disliked this picture at first so it was bought at once by Sir Colin Anderson, then Tate Gallery chairman. Later, after his death, it was presented to the Tate Gallery through his daughter. Sir Frederick now wishes he had the picture.

over, left
Sir Frederick Ashton, OM, 1984   *oil on canvas*   *20 × 24 ins*   THE TATE GALLERY

I was asked to paint this portrait I think because I owned two long-haired golden retrievers like Giles St Aubyn's ones. He was then a housemaster at Eton where I painted the picture.

over, right
The Hon. Giles St Aubyn, c. 1970   *oil on canvas*   *30 × 36 ins*
THE HON. GILES ST AUBYN

110

Isaiah Berlin wrote the introduction to an exhibition of your work at the Marlborough Gallery and said how sheerly enjoyable it was to sit for you, how good the conversation was.

I do like to talk while painting people. It relaxes me and it relaxes them. It allows the personality to come through: I need to be able to *see* the personality coming through: it's a tangible, a visual thing, something that happens while you talk. I work quite fast. I'm not like Lucian Freud or William Coldstream, where there are countless sittings and the sittings take hours and hours. My sitters have to hold the basic pose or they have to go back to it if they wriggle or scratch or something. But within that basic pose I want them to relax, to communicate with me. If a portrait takes too long the spark goes out of it.

What do you feel about Coldstream's or Freud's portraits?

I believe Coldstream painted some of the best portraits of our time. Also the portrait of Julia Strachey by Lawrence Gowing is a masterpiece. I have a drawing for it. But too often I feel with Coldstream that if you stuck a pin into the canvas, so to speak, blood wouldn't run out of his people. Sutherland has painted masterpieces too: the Eddie Sackville-West or the Arthur Jeffress. And I once caused an eyebrow or two to be raised by saying that I thought his portrait of Lord Goodman was like a Giorgione. I'm sure the destruction of the Winston portrait was a disaster, a horrifying loss. I feel Freud is interested in turning people into Freuds: he is a very determining artist though a fine one, like Francis Bacon. I like the portrait of the younger Duchess of Devonshire. It catches her sadness, the sad part of her life or the sad part of her nature. But it doesn't capture the other side, her bounce. How could it? If you make a subject sit too long, or sit too still or too silent, you lose life, immediacy. A critic once said of my portraits that if you saw a lot together it was like straying into a cocktail   → 114

111

112

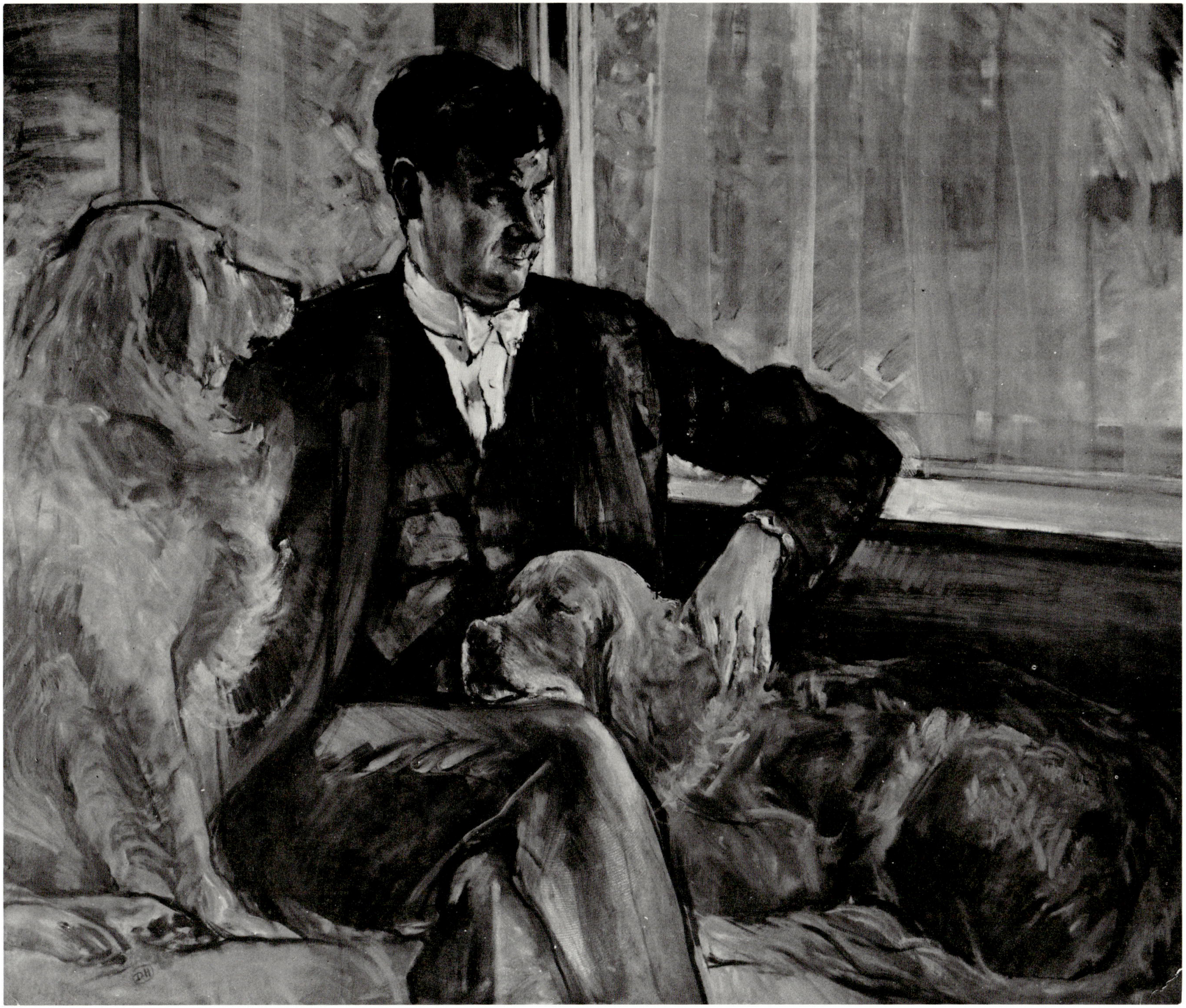

Noël's first remark to me when I painted him in Switzerland was: 'Derek, dear, remember I have painted my own face in the theatre over the last fifty years so know it very, very much better than you ever will.' However he approved of the result and liked it best of the several portraits of him.

Noël Coward, 1968 *oil on canvas*   26 × 30 ins   GRAHAM PAYN

I attempted, in this head of Prince Charles, a Hogarth-type drawing in oils. My earlier portrait of him was done when he was an undergraduate at Trinity. I hope this picture conveys his warm, sensitive and understanding humanity; a concern and interest in whatever he undertakes.

over, left
His Royal Highness the Prince of Wales, 1984   *oil on canvas*   16 × 18 ins
HRH THE PRINCE OF WALES

Probably my most enjoyable sittings were with Sir Isaiah Berlin. The picture was painted at the Warden's Lodgings of All Souls College. Never a dull moment: conversations ranged from theatre in Russia in the thirties to life with Bernard Berenson interspersed with: 'Now do I have my right leg over my left leg or my left leg over my right leg?' from Isaiah.

over, right
Sir Isaiah Berlin, OM, 1973   *oil on canvas*   47 × 39 ins
WOLFSON COLLEGE, OXFORD

114

party: you expected them all to start talking to each other. I think he meant it to be rude. But I didn't mind, I was pleased. Of course there are great portraits which lack immediacy, which are aiming at something quite different: monumentality, perhaps. Perhaps I am making a distinction between portraits and paintings of people. I think that distinction exists.

What about the interplay of emotion in portraiture. Have you ever painted very close friends, or lovers?

Close friends, yes. I don't think I've ever painted lovers because I've had very few lovers.

Do you find it better not to be emotionally involved with the people you paint?

No, not necessarily. I can be emotionally involved, in a way. I mean, sometimes I'm emotionally involved in that I don't like the people and perhaps it shows. I think Sargeant was a great portrait painter, because occasionally you see portraits of people he hated or who hated him. You can tell it at once. I can think of one or two instances like that with me. But in general, I'm a liker: I mean it's exceptional if I don't get on with people. A portrait can also be governed by a strong emotion like admiration. My portrait of the Duke of Buccleuch, the present one, Johnny, not the portrait of Walter, is a case in point. The wheelchair is compositionally very important because his accident has a lot to do with his character, his personality, which I admire. His wife thought I overemphasized it, I believe, but I think it's one of my best portraits. Of course people are sensitive about the way a portrait turns out: the way they look. Likeness is quite a subjective thing, and not everyone agrees about it. Women are especially sensitive, which is why I've painted fewer women.

I find your portraits of women most original, more original perhaps   → 120

115

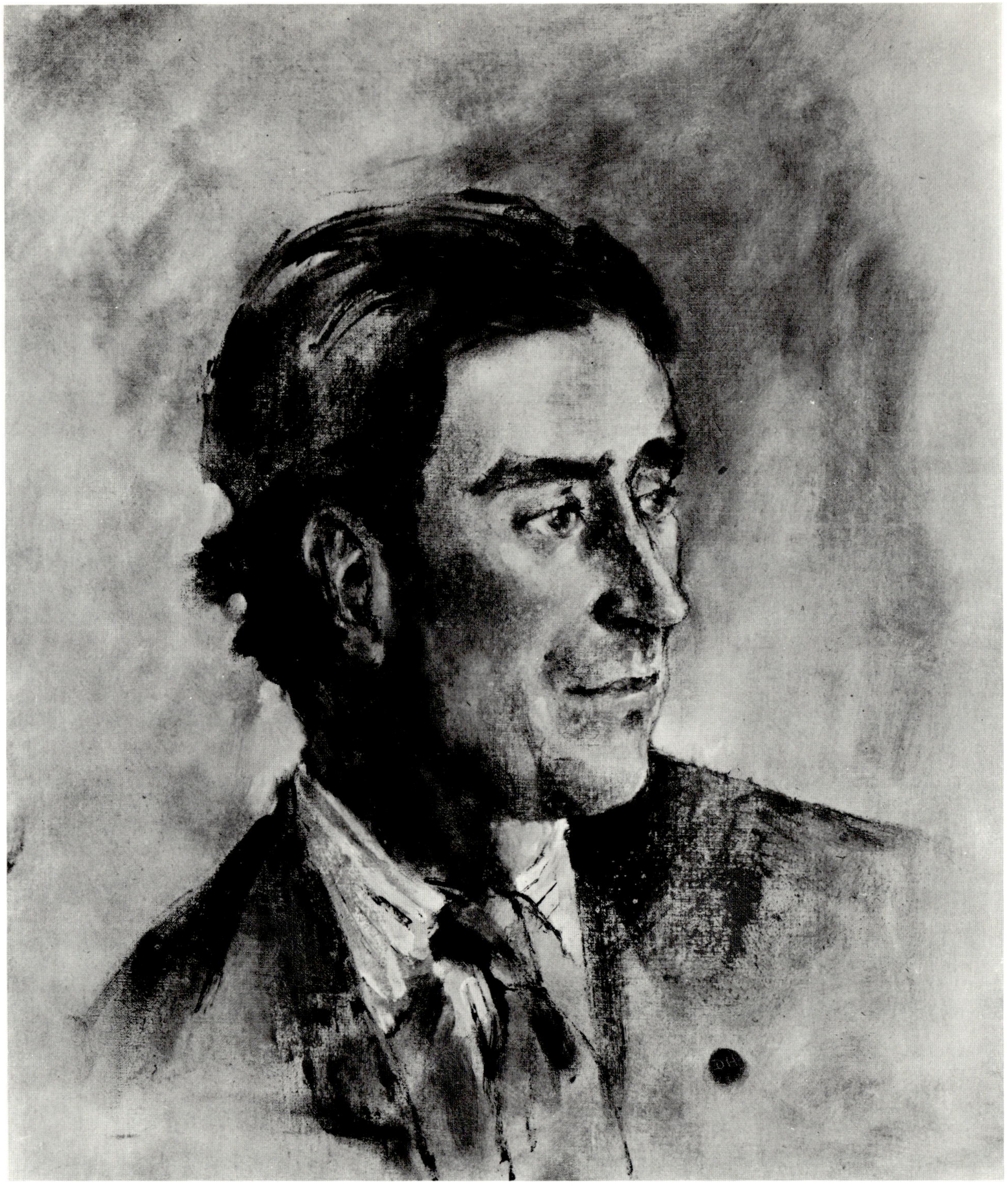

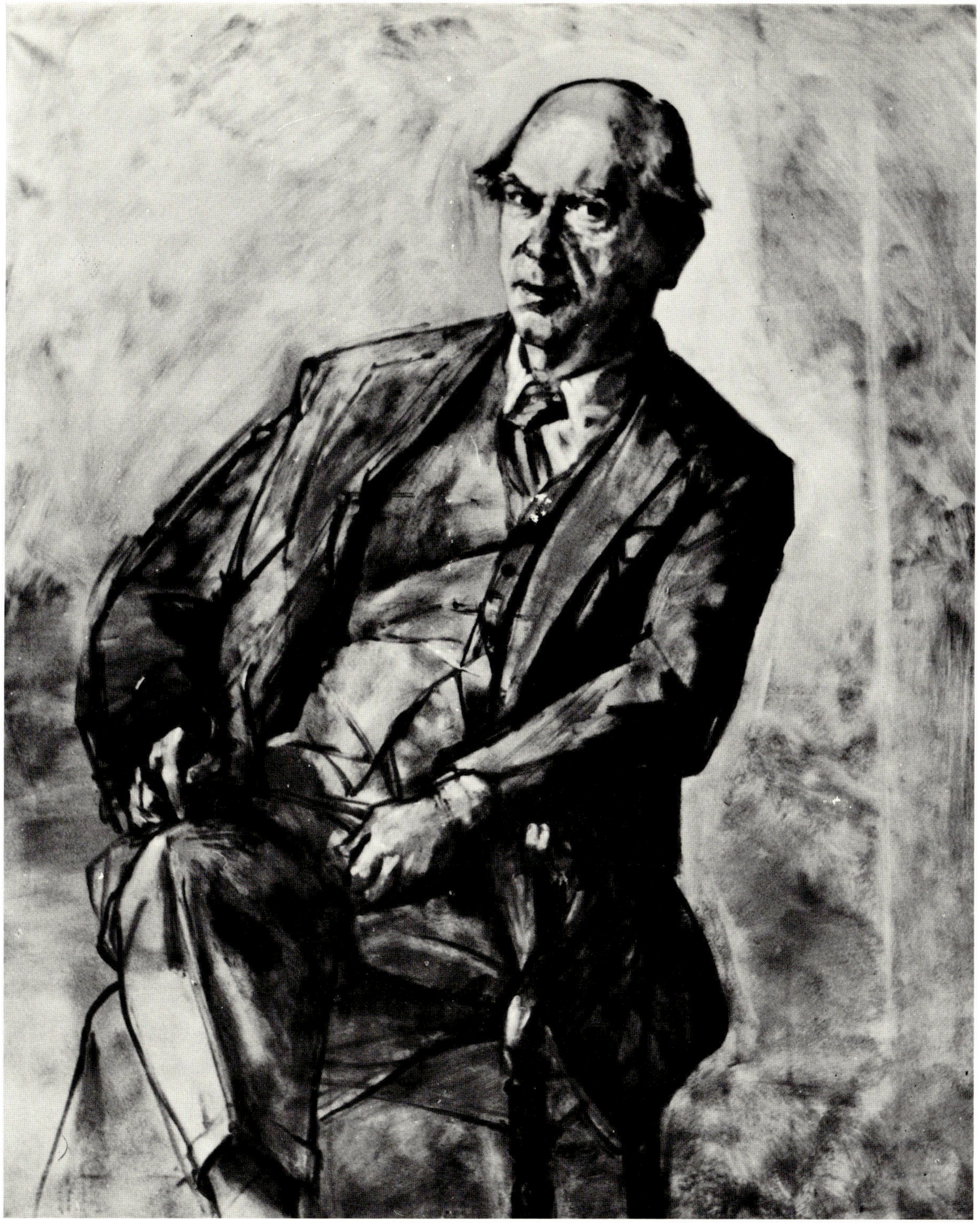

The Earl of Drogheda, the aristocratic and handsome ex-chairman of the *Financial Times*. His wife thought his hair was too untidy and his skin not brown enough as since the picture was finished he had been on a yachting holiday. However, I believe she now likes it and the portrait was used on the jacket of Lord Drogheda's autobiography.

The Earl of Drogheda, 1974   *oil on canvas*   *48 × 28 ins*
THE FINANCIAL TIMES

Nina Toye, the American wife of Francis Toye, who wrote the book on Verdi and was the splendid director of the British Institute in Florence when I was on the board of the Institute during the early 1950s. Two other pictures I did of Nina have unfortunately disappeared also.

Nina Toye, 1950   *oil on canvas*   *24 × 20 ins*   OWNER UNTRACED

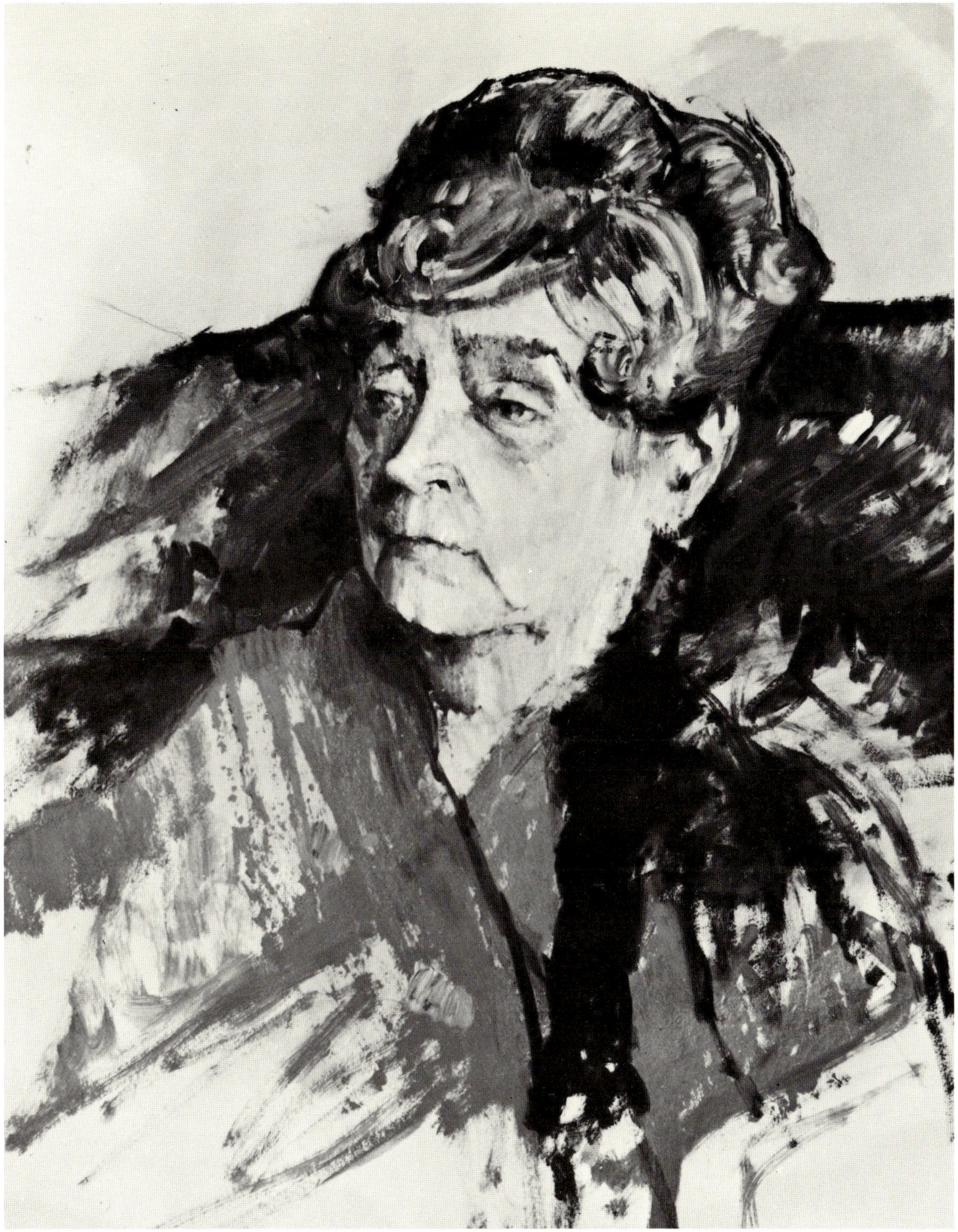

than the male portraits: for example the portraits of Violet Wyndham and Mariga Guinness. It may be that male portraiture still has rather an official air about it: members of boards or college high tables. Or it may be that there are fewer good female portraits in the sense we discussed earlier, as against paintings of models who are female. Nevertheless, and contradicting myself rather, I find two very official portaits among your absolute best: the Cardinal Heard for Balliol and the recent portrait of the present Lord Chancellor for Eton College. Tell me about painting the Lord Chancellor.

I painted him in his office in the House of Lords. It was a delight. I loved him. He couldn't have been a better subject and he was considerate and amusing. It was a chaotic sitting, chaotic in a rather eighteenth-century way, or like a levée in *Rosenkavalier*. There'd be a bang on the door and his secretary would come in and say, 'The President of Malaysia' – or whoever it was – 'to see the Lord Chancellor!' and then the Lord Chancellor would say, 'Oh do come in, I can't get up, I'm being painted. Go and sit over there.' And I would stand twiddling my brush in a corner and then the President would go out and we'd paint for a bit and then there'd be another bang at the door: 'A deputation from Edmonton, Canada, to see the Lord Chancellor!' Or some Indian ladies in saris would be announced and stay for hours. I once asked him, 'Do you enjoy doing all this and having all these people in?' and he said, 'No, not at all, it's Margaret. She doesn't want to see them all herself and she knows I'm one of the ancient sights of London so she sends them along here.'

Yet the portrait works so well. I remember being the first to see it and it taught me something about portrait painting generally. I came to the conclusion that a good portrait painter is one who can trap the visual signals people give about themselves, even if they're not fully aware of the coded information they are giving, so to speak, or have forgotten it.

I think that's true. People present themselves before an audience, even a

Karl Burghardt the great Swiss humanist, diplomat and author painted at the request of Raimund von Hofmannstahl, his godson. Raimund's father, Hugo, and Karl had corresponded and been friends for many years.

Karl Burghardt, 1972 *oil on canvas* 18 × 18 ins MRS KARL BURGHARDT

This picture of an old friend Leslie Hartley, the author, was disliked by a lot of his lady friends who forced him to have a little curtain made to be drawn over it when they visited.

Leslie Hartley, c. 1965 *oil on canvas* 24 × 19½ ins PRIVATE COLLECTION

small one, intuitively. And the intuitive thing works both ways: the painter has to sort out the information in order to understand people and why they look the way they do, their peculiarity. Take the head I painted of Elie Rothschild. Apparently, Elie had one false eye, completely false. I never knew which one it was but in the portrait you can tell immediately. The intuitiveness must be in the looking: you must strip away what you know. I recognize that, in the way of the world, many of my sitters are famous, visually famous in that a lot of people have an idea what they look like. But I have to strip away those associations, which I share, and tackle their likeness in a way that lets what you said, the signals they give, come through. For example, I respect and admire both Prince Charles and my gardener in Donegal immensely. But the image of one is beset by associations and the image of the other isn't. The difficult thing is to get down to looking at each of them properly and to track down, in the mess of the paint itself, the outside and inside of them both.

What about your self-portrait? When did you paint it?

I suppose in my late forties.

It seems to be to be a good and slightly sad picture.

Yes.

It isn't somebody with your immense social gift: it isn't somebody about to throw a party.

No – I hate parties.

It's perhaps the portrait of a traveller.

Yes, a loner.

George Christie still has the air of a slightly mischievous schoolboy. This doubtless helps him in his brilliant direction of the Glyndebourne Opera.

George Christie, 1982   *oil on canvas*   *18 × 18 ins*
SIR GEORGE CHRISTIE

An 'artful dodger' portrait of the good-natured and jovial Lord Hesketh when still a teenager.

Lord Hesketh, 1967   *oil on canvas*   *16 × 16 ins*
THE DOWAGER LADY HESKETH

And are you a loner really?

Very much so. I've never had a satisfactory physical relationship with anyone, ever. I've liked, I've loved people but I've never had a satisfactory, reciprocal relationship, ever.

Does that strengthen you in some ways, here and there?

I wouldn't think so. It may do. I don't really resent it because I've been given so much else in my life, so many privileges in the way of things I've been able to do or see or hear and people I've met. It's just one thing, though an important one, that I happen not to have known.

I certainly believe that the lonely side is, in your case, the force that drives your best work. You touch greatness as a landscape painter and your best landscapes are inspired by one of the loneliest and saddest, as well as most beautiful, parts of the world, the end of the old world, indeed: the west of Ireland. For the purpose of this book I want to end our conversation there. When and why did you go to Ireland?

Well as I've said, I had visited and painted Ireland but I never thought of settling there. Just after the war I painted Achill Island. In 1953 I stayed at Glenveagh Castle in Donegal with Henry McIlhenny. Henry told me about a house nearby, St Columb's. It was an old rectory, a Glebe as the Irish call it. For years it had been a fishing hotel on the Lake of Gartan. It was for sale. I immediately fell in love: it was on a lake, it faced south and the ground fell away from it; it was just the right size and charming architecturally, exactly the sort of house I'd always wanted to live in and the countryside about it was miraculous. As you know, it's gentler, more pastoral country than Glenveagh or Dunlewy and the light shifts even more often, if less dramatically. But the high ground, the bare ground, is there and very near, as you know. I was indecisive; I waited. By the next year the price had →129

James Teacher, a Kentish landowner and former whisky magnate. He is far less severe than I have made him look.

top left
James Teacher, 1985   *oil on canvas*   18 × 18 ins   JAMES TEACHER

Lord Zuckerman. A great scholar and humanist and of course with his zoological connections an animal-lover as well. This was painted in Norfolk where his wife has her studio and depicts the flat marsh landscapes, nearby, so well.

top right
Lord Zuckerman, OM, 1980   *oil on canvas*   18 × 16 ins
LORD ZUCKERMAN, OM

Sir Donald Anderson when head of the P & O shipping firm. He was the brother of Colin Anderson, a Tate Gallery Chairman and a great contributor to the arts in general.

Sir Donald Anderson, 1970   *oil on canvas*   25½ × 30½ ins
P & O STEAM NAVIGATION COMPANY

One of two heads I did of Kenneth (Lord) Clark. This one was for himself and the other for his publisher John Murray. Both were painted when he and his wife Jane had left Saltwood Castle and gone to the Garden House nearby.

Lord Clark writing, 1976 *oil on canvas* *15 × 18 ins*
MISS COLETTE CLARK

Baron Elie de Rothschild. As there were already two portraits of him by Graham Sutherland I was honoured to be asked to depict him again – having already painted his mother-in-law and his brother- and sister-in-law.

Baron Elie de Rothschild, 1984 *oil on canvas* *16 × 20 ins*
BARON ELIE DE ROTHSCHILD

Mary Kessell, a far too little-known artist. I met her through Kenneth Clark who collected and admired her work and from then on she became a near and devoted neighbour to me at the family house in Hampstead. This was painted of her when she stayed on Achill Island in Ireland.

Mary Kessell, 1947 *oil on board*   20 × 20 ins   OWNER UNTRACED

The present Countess of Airlie – this was painted when she was young, but I tried to capture the intensely lively and animated personality she inherited from her mother, the daughter of Otto Kahn. Her grandmother was one of Berenson's closest friends and in the forties we all visited the churches of Venice together in her gondola.

Lady Airlie, 1967 *oil on canvas*   9 × 10¾ ins
THE COUNTESS OF AIRLIE

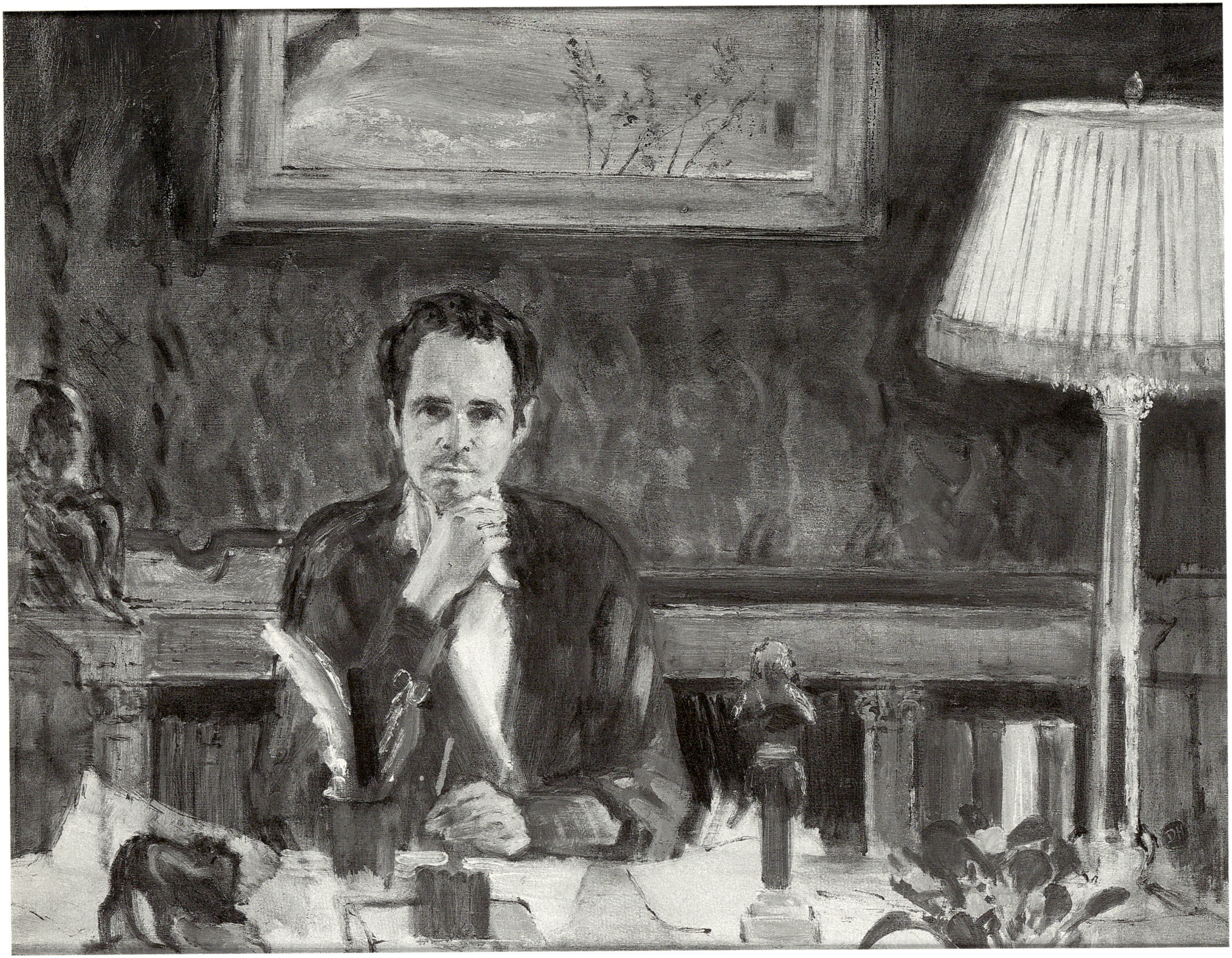

fallen so low I had to buy it. It was incredibly cheap. A thousand pounds for the house and about twenty acres. I've made my home there ever since – or at least until 1981 when I gave it to the Irish nation together with the bulk of my collection and some of my own pictures. They've made a museum in the stables where I had my studio. But I still go back and stay in Donegal, usually with Gracie, my housekeeper.

And like Henry McIlhenny, you made a famous garden there as well.

Nothing on Henry's scale of course. Even allowing for the difference in money, a high romantic garden like Glenveagh wouldn't have been appropriate at Gartan. That's part of the fascination of Donegal, different landscapes, climates even, within a few miles of each other. Glenveagh is a masterpiece; like his art collection, Henry's memorial and a testament to his imagination and verve. My garden was influenced, like my painting, by what I learned in Munich in the thirties from Schwitters and the Bauhaus group. It was all contrast: light against dark, spiky against soft, sunlight against shadow: contrast in the shapes of leaves and plants and in colours. You need such contrast in Ireland or the green overwhelms you. Emphasizing shape was a gift in a way because Donegal isn't famous for flowers but for shrubs. Shrubs give a garden its architecture. They grow well in the mild Gulf Stream atmosphere. So I worked hard at contrast and shape. I wrote an article in the *Horticultural Magazine* on how I planned the garden. Jim Russell was a marvellous help: he would propose the right plants for each prospect. Some of these are dead now, because in spite of the famous Gulf Stream we've had a succession of bitter winters. I worry a bit about the garden, because inevitably the Irish are concentrating on the gallery, the great garden at Glenveagh being so near.

I remember the look of the house inside. It was equally original.

My brother John, the decorator, helped me a lot. He was really

Everett Fahy, former director of the Frick Gallery. I first met him at Berenson's during the early fifties. This picture was painted at my own request on seeing him at his Frick desk below an exquisite Whistler seascape. Unfortunately he disliked the result and I still own this picture.

Everett Fahy, 1978 *oil on canvas* *18 × 24 ins* THE ARTIST

130

responsible for the William Morris revival. We found the original Morris wallpapers I used. Some were serving time as chest-of-drawers lining paper in an Edinburgh boarding house. Morris was much in evidence at Balcarres and Mary Crawford told me where you could find sheets of it. Many of my Islamic things are at St Columb's. It was the time I was travelling regularly, including the journey to Turkey with Freya Stark.

And writing your books on Islamic architecture and decoration?

No. That came later, in the sixties. But when I was in Turkey with Freya in the fifties I bought the extraordinary Turkish wallpapers which in fact were not wallpaper at all, but were used to cover shop windows so that people couldn't window-shop without paying. They mixed well with Morris and since then I've had them copied and transferred to good quality paper in Germany. The originals fade quickly.

The trip with Freya is famous for being less than a triumph.

She mentioned it in her book *Riding to Tigris*. She said 'I parted company with my companion and felt released.'

A stormy relationship?

Not stormy, because I hate storms, except in paintings. I just wrapped myself in cotton wool, cocooned myself, because I was determined not to get angry and to continue our journey. I do want to say how hugely I admire Freya and how devoted I am to her in spite of that journey. It's just the nature of travel, a kind of marriage unless you do it alone: as Freya knows, as Wilfrid Thesiger knows. I'm still doing it. My doctor said I shouldn't but I've just been to South Yemen.

Going back to Ireland, you've painted at Gartan but I think of that → 138

The Duke of Buccleuch in his wheelchair after the agonizing accident that crippled him. His courage and bravery in surmounting such a disaster helped, I feel, to make him into the remarkable character he is – this was the reason I insisted, against fierce opposition, on giving him this pose. It was intended as the very opposite of being disrespectful.

The Duke of Buccleuch, 1973 *oil on canvas* 40¾ × 32½ ins
THE DUKE OF BUCCLEUCH AND QUEENSBERRY, KT

Robin Kenyon Slaney, Shropshire landlord, and for long a near neighbour in Donegal.

Robin Kenyon Slaney, 1972 *oil on canvas*   *18 × 18 ins*   MRS AFIA

Dr Norman Moore, formerly head of St Patrick's Hospital in Dublin, and an outstanding psychologist. Many thousands of patients all over Ireland have been helped by his wonderful understanding of human problems.

Dr Norman Moore, 1979 *oil on canvas*   *18 × 20 ins*
ST PATRICK'S HOSPITAL, DUBLIN

The eldest son and heir of David Somerset, now Duke of Beaufort.

Henry Somerset, 1962   *oil on canvas*   *18 × 12 ins*   THE DUKE OF BEAUFORT

A slight caricature, but not so very exaggerated, of my old friend John Craxton the painter, who lives in Crete and is indistinguishable from many of the citizens in the town of his adoption. A remarkable painter and the most endearing human being.

John Craxton, 1978   *oil on wood*   *5 × 4 ins*   THE ARTIST

Edward Hussey, the eminent Fellow of All Souls, keen ornithologist and visitor to me in Donegal when he came with Warden Sparrow, whom I have also painted several times.

over, left
Edward Hussey, c. 1968   *oil on canvas*   *18 × 24 ins*   JOHN SPARROW

John Grey Murray, one of England's foremost publishers, for whom I have done some six other portraits of his more celebrated authors.

over, right
John Murray, 1977   *oil on canvas*   *20 × 18 ins*   JOHN MURRAY

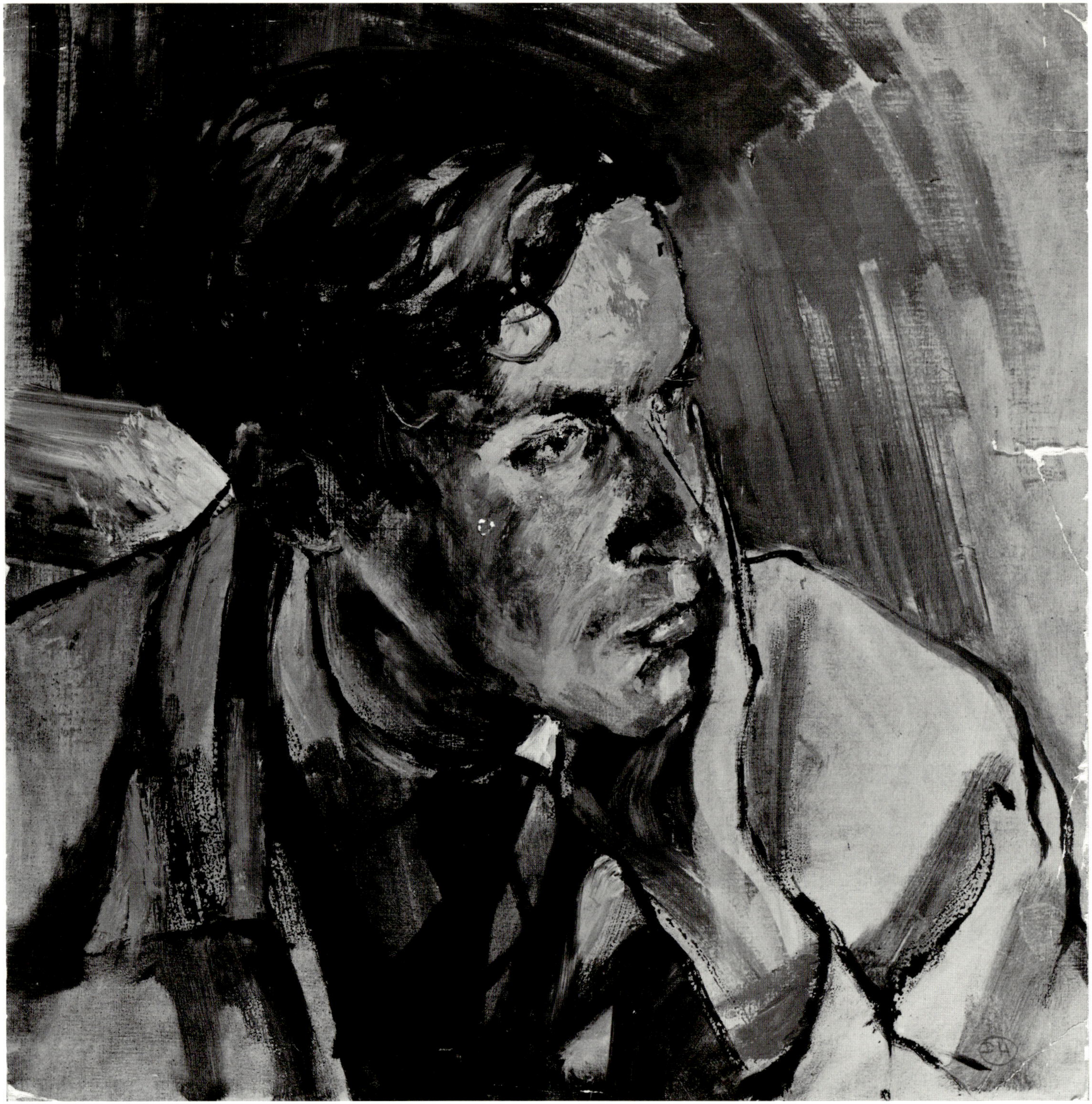

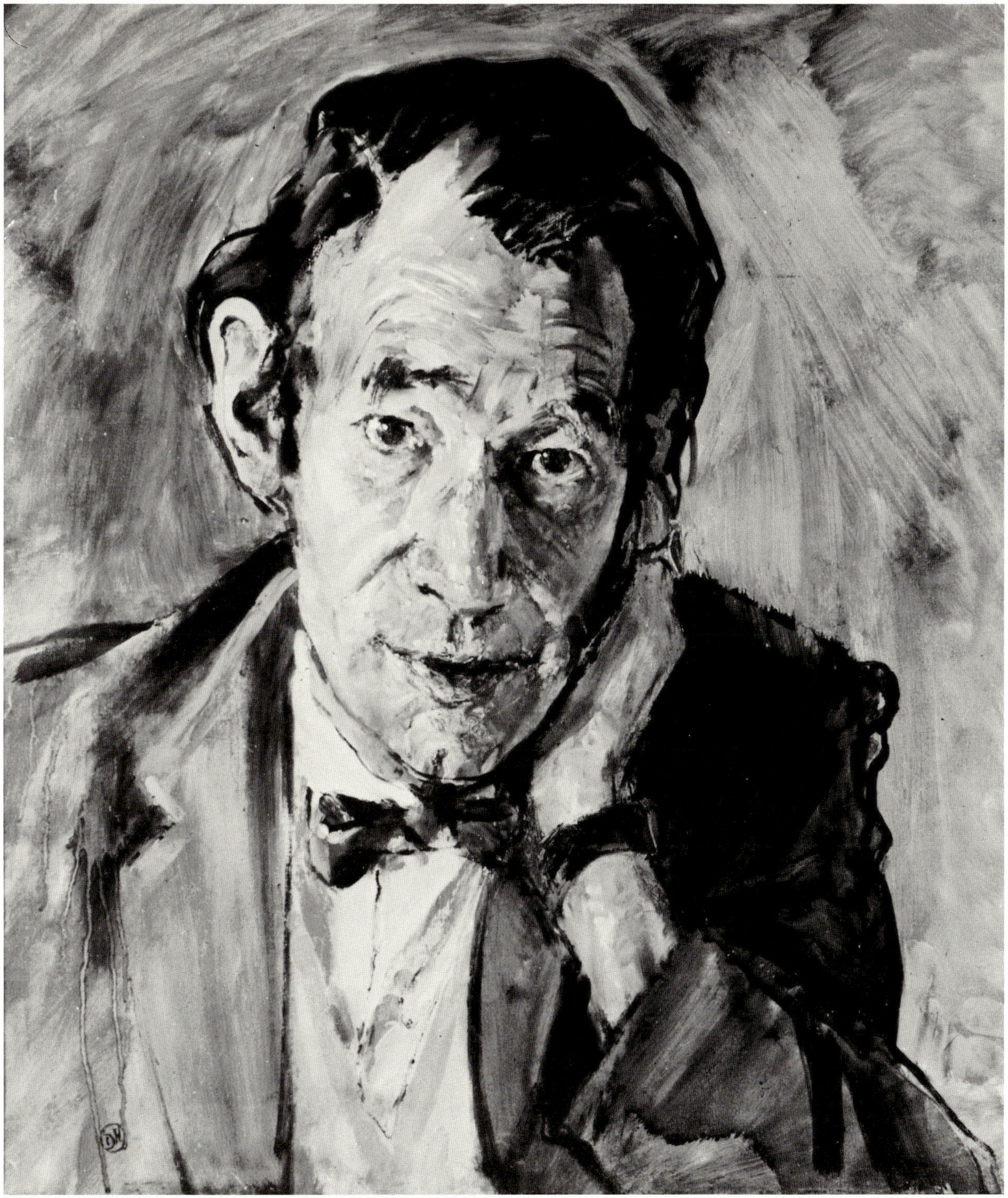

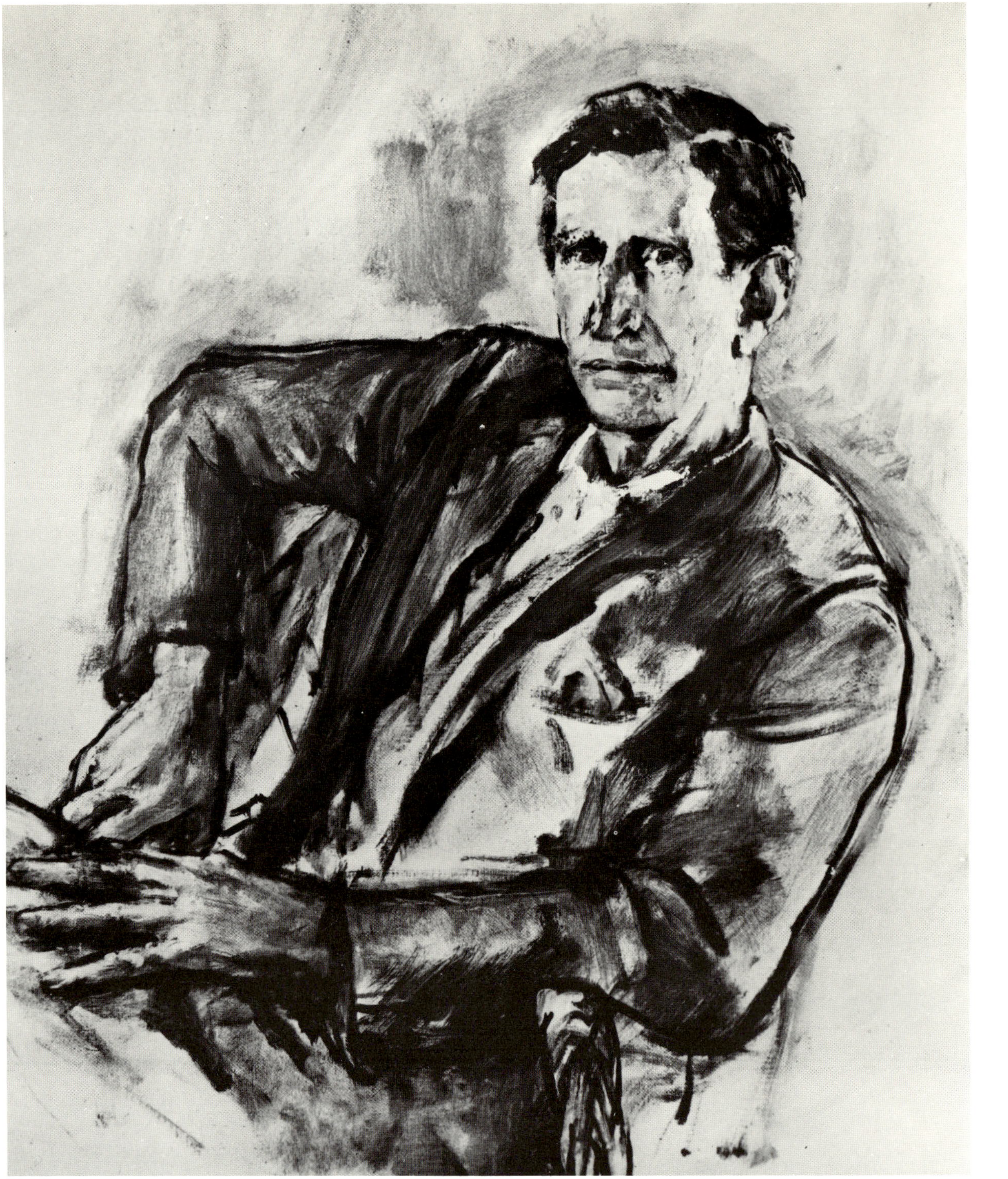

Without doubt one of my best male portraits, Wilfred Thesiger, the explorer. He came to stay with me in Donegal with his mother, a character even more courageous, perhaps, than her renowned son. I did three pictures of Wilfred and his mother liked this one best and always had it near her bed in her own room. When she died, I asked Wilfred where the picture was and after various indecisive letters to and fro it seemed he had asked his brother, former director of Colnaghi's to 'get rid of it'. The final reply I got from his brother in a letter reads: '. . .I gave it to a student, at the Byam Shaw School. . . so that the frame should not be wasted.' In spite of kind enquiries made by the *Sunday Telegraph* and the *Observer*, the picture has never been traced.

Wilfred Thesiger, c. 1973   *oil on canvas*   30 × 26 ins   OWNER UNTRACED

Roger de Candolle, the Geneva-born President of the International Dendrological Society. Also a writer with a splendid book on the Geneva opera.

Roger de Candolle, 1975   *oil on canvas*   20 × 18 ins   ROGER DE CANDOLLE

Prince Jean Louis de Faucigny-Lucinge – also a keen dendrologist and the uncle of Giscard d'Estaing. An old friend for over fifty years – since my Paris student days.

Prince Jean Louis de Faucigny-Lucinge, 1970   *oil on canvas*   20 × 20 ins
PRINCE JEAN LOUIS DE FAUCIGNY-LUCINGE

particular bit of Donegal as a peopled landscape, celebrated also in your portraits of Eddie Moore, the gardener, or John Mangan. As you said, Gartan isn't romantic in feeling like Glenveagh, not so Wagnerian or so like a scene from Doré, but much more of a classical landscape, a damp Italy, with the romantic highlands only a mile or so behind it: a classical landscape set against a romantic one.

Yes, like Claude. The light is like his sometimes.

Now your paintings do have that classical feeling. But when I consider your landscapes I think of you as being two kinds of painter. One is a neo-classicist, sensitive to light and its emotional effects on the viewer, its romantic associations, if you like: a painter who has looked hard at Constable and Corot. The paintings in this category are what Henry McIlhenny called your tiny –

'Derek's tiny postcard masterpieces'. They are done on wood, on cigar box tops mostly.

Yes, and he wasn't being ironic or just teasing because I used to talk to him about them and he had the best eye for French painting in America, which is saying a lot. But there is also the other painter in you. This one is less easy to categorize, less seductive, harsher, more architectural. If one has to compare, then Courbet: the landscapes with rockfaces. A more intense and concentrated Courbet, the landscapes wilder and harsher, a long way from a decent inn.

Yes. It's another side of one's nature. Another side of nature, come to that. For me, the shift has a lot to do with Tory Island. I've had a studio there, just a hut really, for nearly thirty years. I paint there every year. It is the love of getting away alone, and the love of islands. I first went in, I suppose, 1956. I'd met the lighthousekeeper on a train, on the mainland. He told me he was the one person who could help me there as he knew every inhabitant. There was no guest house, but he found me a room with a family in the village. And then I rented the hut. It

Fürstin Gina of Liechtenstein. A small head sketch I did before beginning a state portrait of her husband and herself for the Vaduz Gallery.

top left
Fürstin Gina of Liechtenstein, 1984   *oil on board*   *12 × 10 ins*
THE ARTIST

Giulia Piccini, my Tuscan cook loaned to me by Berenson when I lived in the Villino Corbignano at I Tatti. She and her husband Emilio kept house for me and she was a superb cook quoted in *Italian Food* by Elizabeth David. A larger portrait of Giulia in her Sunday Mass 'mantilla' is in the Graves Gallery, Sheffield.

top right
Giulia Piccini, 1954   *oil on board*   *9 × 7 ins*   THE ARTIST

Princess Tatiana of Hesse. A sketch done of her when staying at Panker, the beautiful Hesse castle in Holstein.

Princess Tatiana of Hesse, 1973   *oil on canvas*   *18 × 18 ins*
HRH PRINCE MORITZ OF HESSE

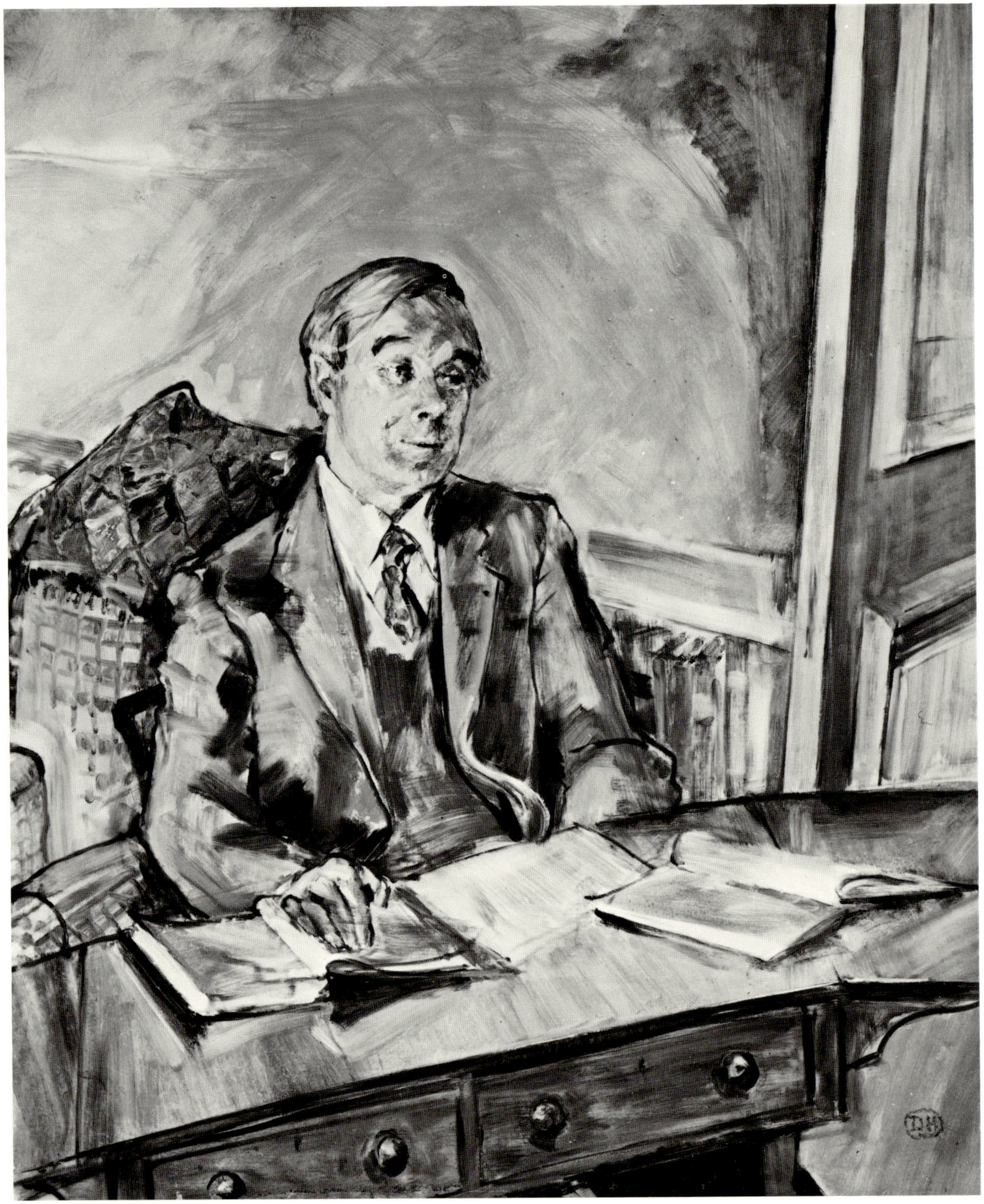

had been put up to monitor shipping during the First World War. I've painted at least 120 pictures there. The weather is finer on Tory than on the mainland, stormier but sunnier. Even when it was too wild to leave the hut, I could usually paint through the window glass. There is no water at the hut. I carry water in buckets each day from the lighthouse. No loo. Rocks. I have a paraffin stove for heat. I can get cabbage on the island and eggs but I take Gracie's bread from home and a cooked leg of mutton which I keep in the lighthouse fridge. Tory is very small now. The population has declined since the fifties. It has about 150 people now. There were nearly 300 when I first went. Halved. It would be a crime if it were evacuated, as they say it might be. It is at the edge of the old world, an important outpost of civilization. St Columba went there. The islanders live on fishing and government grants and cousins in America.

Your paintings of Tory are austere. I've never had the feeling that you allow the interest and romance of the place, the literary atmosphere so to speak, to intrude. There's nothing Celtic Revival about them, or Synge's Riders to the Sea, *as you said –*

No: it's visual, but I hope the isolation, the harshness is there. In the same way the Burren is one of my favourite parts of Ireland. No one else has painted it.

Unless you count Richard Long: the Walk in Ireland *looks like the Burren. But you also created a school of painters on Tory, did you not?*

They were there already. They just didn't paint. Jimmy Dixon saw me painting and came up and said he could do better. And I said, 'Yes. Why don't you?' and gave him stuff to paint with. In the end he'd make his own brushes out of a donkey's tail. He was the most prolific painter. His brother started when he saw that Jimmy was making money out of the paintings. He was as good, but he did only →144

Sir Alan Hodgkin. Painted for the Royal Society when he was President of that Society. It seems they resented the fact that the paint was not thick enough! At one moment his black cat leapt on to his table and would have been perfect for the composition of the picture. However, we agreed the august society might not have liked that either.

Sir Alan Hodgkin, OM, 1975 *oil on canvas* 50 × 40 *ins* THE ROYAL SOCIETY

Sir Sarvepalli Radhakrishnan, that great President of India. A picture commissioned by All Souls College where he was a Fellow. A most remarkable man of integrity, simplicity and dignity as well as learning. He seemed to me to be a mixture of Gandhi and Berenson, and I loved the sittings with him in Lutyens' great viceregal building in Delhi. Swallows nesting in his room flew in and out and all pomp and ceremony were absent.

Sir Sarvepalli Radhakrishnan, OM, 1967 *oil on canvas* 47½ × 37½ *ins*
ALL SOULS COLLEGE, OXFORD

Sir Steven Runciman. The picture was full-length when offered to the National Portrait Gallery. They tactfully and rightly suggested the picture might be cut to waist-level. I agreed with this and did so – only to have the result refused and returned to me! Perhaps one of my best likenesses.

top left
Sir Steven Runciman, CH, 1970   *oil on canvas*   18 × 20 ins   THE ARTIST

The chef at The Marlborough Club in Pall Mall before it closed down for ever.

top right
The Chef, *c.* 1960   *oil on canvas*   24 × 14½ ins   THE VISCOUNT HAMBLEDEN

A sketch, done on a bit of old packing board, of Sir Osbert Lancaster. The later portrait of him is owned by his publishers John Murray. A man who gave enjoyment and laughter to his painter as well as to his readers.

Sir Osbert Lancaster, *c.* 1972   *oil on wood*   17 × 16½ ins   LADY LANCASTER

143

about five pictures in his life. Then there was Jimmy Rogers, who'd started painting in America. He was very good but also not prolific. Another one painted five or six brilliant pictures and then one Sunday after Mass he disappeared and was never seen again.

Drowned?

I suppose so. And now there is a second generation of painters, three or four of them. They have exhibited in Paris. Jimmy Dixon had an exhibition in Vienna –

Are they as good?

I don't think so, yet, but they may become as good. The interesting thing is that they are hard-edge painters, they like hard linear effects whereas the older ones were Impressionists. Strange that they should have switched to a kind of hard-edge Hockney effect without ever having seen a Hockney.

So you aren't too isolated on Tory?

Only on purpose. I need the isolation, though of course the landscape is never still, with all that action of sea and air. I like people. I need to be stimulated by people. But I cannot have a day without the need to spend several hours entirely alone. Every day, and it goes through all my life too.

Biographical Note

1916
Born in Southampton.

1929
To school at Marlborough.

1933
Left school and travelled to Munich to study stage design. Worked from the model and studied Bauhaus principles.

1935
To Paris for six months to work at stage design with Paul Colin. Met many artists in Paris and became increasingly absorbed by Braque, Juan Gris and French nineteenth-century painting. Designed sets and costumes for Rameau's *Castor and Pollux* produced by the Oxford University Opera Club at Oxford.

To Vienna to study design with Dr Josef Gregor, head of the National Theatre collection. Did very little painting, concentrating on stage design. Constantly drew from life at the Kunstgewerbe School.

First journey to Italy, to Florence.

While in Vienna designed sets and costumes for *Agamemnon*, under Dr Gregor's auspices, at the Burg Theatre, but Nazi occupation stopped the production.

1936
To Russia, to study theatre design in Moscow, Leningrad and Kiev. Became interested in early Russian frescoes and ikons. A journey across Siberia to Japan, then visiting Peking, Bali, Angkor and Siam, making many drawings.

1937

London: sets and costumes for Frederick Ashton's ballet *The Lord of Burleigh*, with music by Mendelssohn, at Sadler's Wells.

1938

To Paris, and settled in a studio in rue Campagne Première. Encouraged by Edward Molyneux, gradually abandoned the idea of stage design and began to paint. A classical taste was formed, but considerable sympathy for Bonnard, Vuillard and Picasso.

Rented an old mill on the Loire and studied and painted the landscape of the district.

1939

England: the artist worked on a farm in Hampshire and painted in his spare time, an arrangement which continued till 1945.

Met Keith Vaughan, John Minton, Mary Kessell and other artists in England. Influenced by Palmer and Sutherland, the writings of Geoffrey Grigson, and in touch with Victor Pasmore, Lawrence Gowing – who lived nearby in Wiltshire, Coldstream and other Euston Road painters.

Some essays published in John Lehmann's *New Writing* magazine on the theatre in Russia and the Chinese threatre, and the Greek influence in Russian art. Some paintings are reproduced in this periodical.

1940

Began to depart from strict observation of nature in his work and became increasingly interested in construction and design. In this, the artist learned much from Victor Pasmore.

Exhibited in 'Nine Painters' show at Reid and Lefèvre with Geoffrey Tibble, Quentin Bell, Colin MacInnes and others. Edward Marsh, secretary to Sir Winston Churchill, bought one of his pictures for the Contemporary Art Society.

1943

First one-man show at the Nicholson Gallery.

1944

Organized 'Constable to Cézanne' exhibition at Wildenstein's Gallery.

1945

Organized second exhibition at Wildenstein's Gallery: 'Since the Impressionists'.

1946

To Ireland, where the artist lived for a year, painting in Galway, Mayo and on Achill Island, studying the sea, cliffs and rocks. Fascinated by Stephen Gwynne's book *La Source d'Art* on the Scythian influence in Celtic art and the Scythian infiltration into Ireland. The illustrations, by Marie Howet, with facsimiles of gouaches of the Irish landscape and their feeling for its structure greatly influenced the artist.

From 1946 to 1960 contributed occasional essays to the *New Statesman*, as well as *New Writing, The Burlington Magazine, Apollo,* etc.

1947

One-man show at the Leicester Galleries.

Sets and costumes for *Il Trovatore* at Covent Garden.

1948

To Italy. Lectured at Verona on 'England and Impressionism'.

1949
Returned to Italy and travelled extensively, painting and drawing. Showed work to Berenson who encouraged him and invited him to live in the Villino at I Tatti during the winter months of the next five years. Studied Italian old masters and made paintings of the city of Urbino. Reviews for the *Times Literary Supplement*, *Burlington Magazine*, *Observer* and *Spectator*.

Met Guttuso, Music, Dalla Zorza, Saetti, and Morandi, for whom the artist has a special admiration.

1950
Settled in a house on Holly Hill, Hampstead. Second one-man show at Leicester Galleries.

1951
Lectures for the British Council in South Italy and Sicily; appointed to the Board of Governors of the British Institute in Florence.

1952
Organized a Degas exhibition for the Edinburgh Festival, later shown at the Tate Gallery. Visited Matisse for a BBC broadcast.

1953
Appointed Art Director at the British School at Rome, where the artist worked during the winters of the following two years.

1954
Bought a house in Donegal, where the artist has spent most of his time since this date.

Met Jack Yeats, in Ireland, for whom the artist had a strong sympathy.

A journey to Eastern Turkey, with Freya Stark.

1956
Awarded a prize in the 'Seasons' exhibition organized by the Contemporary Art Society at the Tate Gallery.

1957
Art Director at the British School at Rome for another two years. Among the students at the time were Henry Inlander, Derrick Greaves, Joe Tilson, John Bratby, Michael Andrews and Norman Norris. Exhibited at L'Obelisco Gallery in Rome.

From this year painted regularly in Donegal and on Tory Island as well as in Italy.

1958
Became a member of the Committee of the Contemporary Art Society.

Second journey to Turkey.

A photographic survey commenced of early Islamic architecture.

1960
Another journey in connection with the survey of Islamic architecture, visiting Turkey, Persia, Afghanistan, Samarkand and Bokhara. Exhibited Tory Island pictures in Dublin and Belfast.

1961
Organized Landseer Exhibition at The Royal Academy with John Woodward. Portrait commissions, including John Sparrow, Warden of All Souls, Oxford. Retrospective Exhibition at the Whitechapel Art Gallery, London, organized by Bryan Robertson.

1963
Private show of portraits at Admiral's House, Hampstead, home of Sir Colin Anderson, the then Chairman of the Tate Gallery.

1965
Published with Professor Oleg Grabar *Islamic Architecture and Its Decoration*.

1976
Published with L. Golvin *Islamic Architecture in North Africa*.

1978
Exhibition of Portraits at Marlborough Fine Art (London) Ltd. First London exhibition since Whitechapel Retrospective in 1961.

1980
Journey to North Yemen for proposed book on architecture.

1982
Eight pictures stolen in Liverpool.

1985
Journey to North and South Yemen for proposed book on architecture.

Works by Derek Hill are in the following public collections

Arts Council of Great Britain
Tate Gallery
Bagshaw Art Gallery, Batley, Yorkshire
City Art Gallery, Bradford
City Art Gallery, Carlisle
City Art Gallery, Southampton
University College, Swansea
Art Gallery and Museum, Worksop
Birmingham City Art Gallery
National Portrait Gallery of Ireland, Dublin
Sir Hugh Lane Municipal Gallery of Modern Art, Dublin
Museum and Art Gallery, Belfast
Berenson Foundation, Florence
National Gallery of Canada, Ottawa
Fogg Art Museum, Harvard University, Cambridge, Mass., USA
Birmingham Gallery, Alabama, USA
National Portrait Gallery, London
Walker Art Gallery, Liverpool
National Portrait Gallery of Denmark

The Philadelphia Museum of Art, USA
Gallery of Modern Art, Edinburgh
Herbert Gallery, Coventry
Graves Gallery, Sheffield